Tape Reading
&
Market Tactics

Tape Reading
&
Market Tactics

BY HUMPHREY B. NEIL

Marketplace Books
Columbia, Maryland

CONTENTS

FROM THE PUBLISHER
(2007 Edition)

How can a publisher of trading books not be fascinated by the 1920s? Radio, cars, airplanes—machines of every sort fueled the hype machine leading up to that black Tuesday in 1929, much like maniacal statements of "Twenty five year run!" that wafted about like cigar smoke in Manhattan's fashionable East Side during the 1990s. You could still smoke in bars in New York's financial section back then, but that's perhaps the only thing that has changed. Our trading pitfalls surely haven't.

The author of this book spent most of his life analyzing the trends inherent in the stock market. He took an entirely contrarian view, saying that most people are pulled like sheep at the beck and call of media moguls, breaking news flashes, and the general "buzz" of the Wall Street zoo. A contrarian himself, Neill was a tried and true Vermont realist and his practical New England style would have nothing of unwarranted speculation. As he says in the book, "In all that I shall have to say, I warn you that I see on the tape only the results of buyers' and sellers' transactions in stocks; mine are not eyes that perceive the occult signs of movements of J.P. Morgan and Company or short sales executed by Jesse Livermore."

This was the insight and philosophy of a studied academic, one who pushed his readers to study hard and pay their dues. He insisted that the successful trader is his own person: an entrepreneur and, collectively, a real and powerful influence on the market. But he balanced his motivational text with a tested dose of reality. He said that we simply cannot dance the dance of the huge money brokers who pull the puppet strings, but we can read their actions—down to each minute detail on tape and we react to those actions as necessary. Coming from the debacle of 1929, he added to this process the powerful notion of limited losses. In essence, he gave us the makings of a plan—one where we balance gains against losses in a way that breeds rational expectations of success. This message of setting realistic trading goals is beyond all, a priceless gift to take away from this book.

So the concept of staying to a plan, or at least a set emotional course in trading, can be considered one of the backbones of Neill's work. In the end, he warned us to accept the human system as it is and work within it and against it at the same time. Most important though, don't get pulled into the frenzy of the next "big trade." As he concluded, " Take it from the Market Philosopher: human nature in the stock market is going to be the most profitable study in the next bull market... Many a healthy reaction has proved fatal."

All of this is why Humphrey B. Neill's book remains a powerful influence more than seven decades after its first publication in 1931. Neill hammered down the message that herd mentality is the aphrodisiac of the trading mind, drawing on emotions and pushing its fatal impulses. All the standard evils are outlined in this work, from greed and ego to the weakness of thinking you'll make easy money in the market. Neill made a statement to his generation: don't follow the crowd. The answer, he said, is in reading the tape. Follow it. Master it. And above all, do not become a pawn in what is probably the most predictably unpredictable game in the world...the stock market.

PREFACE
(February, 1931)

In the making of this book, the tail literally has wagged the dog. The original plan was to collect in bound form a number of editorials written and published in a little magazine called *If, As and When.* As I set about coordinating and editing these various manuscripts, the thought presented itself that every speculator has three steps to climb before he can expect consistent market success.

These are: first, familiarizing himself with the power and the methods of the professional speculative groups which operate "behind the tickers;" second, learning the principles whereby he may interpret the maneuvers of those groups and the actions of the public; and third—and most important—attaining a mastery of himself: of his temperament, emotions, and the other variables that go to make up human nature.

In conference with the publishers, it was then decided to make the main portion of this book a treatise on the interpretation of the ticker tape, inasmuch as there have been any number of inquiries about, and requests for, instruction in tape reading and market tactics. Consequently the reader will find this volume divided into three parts: the first being a brief review of stock speculation; the second the above-mentioned treatise, and the third a group of selections from what was to have been the whole—the plan being thus designed to cover the three steps to successful stock trading.

Candidly, I tackled the task with a fair amount of stage fright, realizing that for many years no book had been published on the subject of interpreting market movements from the action as revealed on the ticker tape, and, also, because I have been told by many traders that what they learn from the tape comes to them only after years of experience, which has finally given them a "second sight" or intuitive eye. I am not insensible to this belief; but I am convinced that any intelligent person with, perhaps, an extra grain or two of common sense and mental agility can learn in a comparatively short time to tell from the tape what is likely to happen.

Right here, however, I should like to inject my personal opinion that anyone who attempts to catch the hourly, or even daily, fluctuations of stock prices is entering upon a risky, foolhardy enterprise. There may be some traders who have made, and are making, money from these so-called scalping operations; but I have never met one who was successful for long. In talks with brokers I have been told again and again that the "in-and-out" trader speculating "for a turn" lasts but a few months. The reader will find arguments to substantiate this view throughout the following pages.

It must be recognized that there are methods of gauging the manipulative and speculative forces in the market other than that of reading the stock ticker tape. To many, the thought of tape reading is sinister and reeks of gambling. These same persons, however, will listen to tips and will scan brokers' letters and the financial papers in the hope of hitting upon some commitment whereby they will reap a fat profit.

The tape records the prices at which buyers and sellers have met and agreed upon exchanges of stocks for money. This same record may be printed upon sheets or grouped for a day's business and published in the newspaper. It may be recorded upon charts. What are the odds? Some speculators—and everyone who buys common stocks with the expectation of some time selling at higher prices is a speculator—may wish to draw their conclusions from the tape; others may never have the time to look at a ticker and may depend upon other forms of records. There is no quarrel here: each one must decide for himself from whence he secures his data.

There is this to be said against constant tape watching: unless the trader has secure control of himself there is the grave danger of his perspective's becoming too confined and of his placing too much importance upon minor details within the various days' records. The middle road appears, without question, to be the most profitable for the average, conservative speculator. If he travels this path he will turn to the tape only upon occasions, and will retain a clear head for the broader objectives ahead, rather than have his eyes and mind glued on the confusion of near-by objects rushing past him.

The principles of analyzing market action are the same, whether employed to interpret short-term trading trends, or followed in order to determine the extent of the far safer intermediate trends which last for anywhere from three weeks to six months.

There are any number of books published which relate to other forms of market interpretation: chart reading, statistical studies, fundamentals, and other factors. All have their advantages and good points. It certainly is conceded that one cannot have too much knowledge of the forces which "make the market." Recent years have demonstrated that the public generally knows little of what actually happens within the realms of common-stock speculation.

The emphasis throughout this book is upon the human equation as it relates to market action. I have attempted to make stand out in relief the difficulties besetting the speculator and to discuss informally many factors of stock speculation which have been practically ignored in other books. The principles are not new; in fact, I believe them to be behind the accepted practice of all successful speculators. I hope, however, that the presentation is helpfully different and that it will bring into sharper focus the important problems which must be solved if we are to trade in the market with profitable results.

In accumulating and selecting the material for this book I have drawn heavily upon the experience of others. I only wish that I might thank each person individually for whatever share he has contributed. That would be impossible without listing hundreds of men with whom I have had the pleasure of discussing the market. Likewise, I am indebted in large measure to the thousands of correspondents whose letters of inquiry on investment matters I have read and studied. These experiences have aided in the development of an understanding of the public's mind and of how the public acts in the market.

I owe to my associates in business more than I shall be able to repay; but I thank them for the privilege of absorbing much knowledge from their economic, statistical, and graphic studies. In particular, I tender thanks to Buchanan Tyson and Arnold W. Wetsel for many of the ideas expressed within these pages, and for their generous aid and suggestions at all times.

To Richard W. Schabacker, Harold C. Wolcott, and Howard M. Cool, I am also greatly indebted for their patient reading and constructive criticism of the manuscript. And I wish to acknowledge with gratitude the work of Stanley W. Mahon in drawing the charts and of Miss Charlotte Quasebarth in correcting and typing the manuscript.

To the reader, I acknowledge full responsibility for the views and opinions expressed herein, and hand him this book with sincere humility, knowing full well the danger which lies in offering any text on "how to do it." No system of forecasting the movements of stock prices ever can be infallible. However, there are many pitfalls in speculation which may be avoided; and it is my hope that somewhere within these pages the reader will find hints and suggestions which will enable him to "dodge the crowd" and forever resign his membership in that great club, The Public, after which title there is added, in stock market circles, the epithet "always wrong."

New York City, February, 1931
Humphrey B. Neill

PART ONE
STOCK SPECULATION

Chapter 1

Stock Speculation

Before we launch into our study proper, let us first review our ABC's.

What is the stock market? It is simply a marketplace for the exchange of certificates for money, or money for certificates. In the world of securities speculation, stock certificates hold the same place as, say, cloaks and suits do in the cloak-and-suit trade: they are merchandise, to be bought and sold for profit. Whereas the cloak-and-suit manufacturer buys cloth from which he makes his merchandise, the financial "manufacturer" (called "underwriter" or "banker") seeks situations for which he may manufacture stock certificates. Many plans of refinancing have been initiated by the financial community when their shelves have been bare of merchandise. They must sell stocks or they cannot earn profits.

In addition to the manufacturers, there are others who do no underwriting, but act solely as distributors of stocks; and others still who limit their business to buying and selling for their own purposes.

When common stocks possess certain qualifications, their listing is permitted upon the New York Stock Exchange. In addition, there are thousands of issues listed upon the other exchanges. I shall devote the discussions in this book to the New York Stock Exchange, although the principles will hold good in nearly all speculative situations.

Who makes the purchases and sales of stocks so listed? Let me group them roughly into three divisions:

1. Investors seeking income. Institutions (insurance companies, industrial corporations, trusts, etc.) Banks' investment affiliates. Investment trusts (those which actually invest).

2. Businessmen speculators, brokerage-office traders, and the other thousands of amateurs who trade in the hope of making easy money; also, trading trusts and corporations.
3. Professional operators, stock exchange floor traders, pools, investment bankers, and other *intelligent* speculators.

We shall here be concerned chiefly with groups two and three, the speculators; for group one, the investors, could not possibly buy a fraction of the stocks which are exchanged in one day alone. For instance, during an active day's trading 150,000 shares of United States Steel common stock may be exchanged at an average price of $200 per share, this by itself would total $30,000,000. In order to give some idea of the magnitude of the value of the stocks listed on the New York Stock Exchange, I shall remind you that by November, 1930, nearly forty billions of dollars had been sheared from their value as represented by the prices at which those stocks had been selling only a little more than a year previous.

I am emphasizing this because, if we are to appreciate the important place speculation holds in our present financial set-up, we must realize the gigantic task which the speculative element shoulders.

The United States Steel Corporation, as of September 30, 1930, reported that the holdings of their investors were 7,056,679 common shares, or 81.04 percent of the total outstanding capitalization. This compares with investors' holdings of 74.75 percent on September 30, 1929, and shows an unusual gain during that year, no doubt due in large part to many marginal traders taking up their stock in full during and after the breaks.

As of September 30, 1930, there were 1,612,599 shares in the hands of brokers and speculators. This compares with 2,034,512 shares in 1929. In other words, assuming an average price of $150 per share and an average floating supply of around 2,000,000 shares, which was the average for the four years prior to 1930, you will note that the speculators and brokers alone carried some $300,000,000 worth of the common stock of United States Steel Corporation.

Many corporations pointed with pride to their increased numbers of stockholders during 1930. E. I. Du Pont de Nemours and Company, a conspicuous one among them, disclosed the interesting fact that the number of their stockholders had increased from 24,134 to 32,683, as of October 31, 1930. These stockholders held an average of 28 shares each. No indication was given, of course, that this increase also may have been caused, as in Steel and many other corporation, by large numbers of our group two who during the decline became involuntary investors.

How many of these involuntary investors will become speculators again when stock prices rise? I leave this problem to you to solve definitely. However, I am certain that thousands of people who say, today: "Never again; I'll own my stocks outright after this," will very shortly forget their depression-year resolutions and be back for more profits—or punishment.

The stock market is a great cauldron of the hopes, desires, and despairs of speculators, or traders. If it were not for the speculators, there would be no active stock·market. If it were not for the speculators, America would not stand where she does, as the leading industrial country in the world. We may deplore speculation, but if it were not for this outpouring of money for stocks, you and I should not enjoy a fraction of the comforts and luxuries which we accept as necessities.

The speculators "carry the ball" until the goal is reached; that is to say, speculators keep stocks afloat until they sink into the strong-boxes of investors.

We all know that there is a constant battle being waged between the professionals of group three, and the amateurs of group two, otherwise known as "the public."

The public is the customer to whom the professional trader or the financial manufacturer hopes to sell his product. As competition is the life of commerce, so is it the life of speculation. The speculatively-minded public hopes to make money by trading in stocks in a hit-or-miss manner, while the professional strives for his profits through engineering his maneuvers so scientifically that the public will take from him property which he has acquired at lower prices.

Unless we who make up the public have a thorough knowledge of why the professional exists and how he operates, we cannot hope to win in our engagements with him.

First, let us look into group three more closely and break it down, in order to differentiate between the various types. The investment banker (or any banking organization that underwrites, or purchases, stocks or bonds from one who needs capital) is the manufacturer and distributor. As we have seen, he is the same as a cloak-and-suit manufacturer, in that he must sell the goods he has fabricated before he can make his profit.

The stock-and-bond manufacturer may employ from time to time other distributors, high-pressure sales managers (pool operators), and may appoint any number of agents to sell for him throughout the world. He often receives aid from stock brokers also, and from their legions of salesmen (customers' men). The pool operators accumulate stocks when, in their judgment, they are cheap, with the expectation of selling them to us, the public, later at higher prices.

Besides these members of the professional speculative element, there are the many important, individual traders, who buy and sell stocks for their own accounts, depending upon their own wits, skill, and judgment to make money out of their buying and selling operations; to say nothing of many other persons performing functions not immediately pertinent to our study. The ramifications of the manufacturing and distributive system for stocks and bonds are probably more intricate than those of any other commercial pursuit.

The professional may be called in as a specialist in any one of a number of situations. A manufacturer of bathroom fixtures may wish to raise capital with which to build a new plant, but before issuing more stock he calls upon the financial manufacturer.

This specialist may advise him that before he actually issues the new stock it would be wise to arrange for a more active market in his present stock, for then he can sell his new stock at higher prices. Therefore, the plans are worked out similarly to the plans which would be carried out if the manufacturer were planning to market a new line of his own merchandise, bathroom fixtures.

The professional may be called in by a group of large stockholders of a given corporation who wish to sell their stock, but who realize that they cannot all offer their holdings for sale simultaneously without breaking the price of the stock. The professional will undertake to sell their stock for them to the public, and his agreement with the stockholders will be to obtain a given average price.

A number of professionals may bank together—form a pool—for the purpose of acquiring a quantity of a stock which they think may be marketed to the public at a higher price.

One company may wish to gain control of another company through open market acquisitions of the stock. It may need, for example, only 50,000 shares to gain a working control. A professional may be called in to act as the purchasing agent. In this instance his tactics will be reversed. It will be his job to buy cheaply, rather than to sell dearly. His tactics will be to depress the stock in price in order to persuade the public to sell.

There are any number of examples which I might give to demonstrate the reasons for the existence of the professional. The thought to bear in mind is that the business of the financial community is to sell stocks to the public. There is a purpose behind every operation by a professional: it may be simply an individual campaign for personal profit; or, it may be a well conceived plan for the raising of capital for industry. As soon as we appreciate that the professional element looks upon us as customers, rather than as partners, we shall begin to perceive the task we face in attempting to make money by trading in stocks or, incidentally, even by investing in stocks.

Now let me turn back a moment in order that we may see the methods by which a professional gains his ends.

Let us assume, for the sake of an example, that a number of us believe that the common stock of the Amalgamated Motor Car Company is cheap at prevailing prices. We are acquainted with the officials of the company, who tell us that their business is picking up, that certain things point to larger profits in the near future. They advise us further, confidentially, that the directors are planning a pleasant surprise for their stockholders, and expect to capitalize a portion of the huge surplus which has been built up; in other words, we learn that a stock dividend is pending.

Upon investigation, we find that there are only three large stockholders who would be likely to sell any quantity of stock; and with these we make arrangements whereby they give us options on their stock at prices considerably above the current market. We are now prepared to accumulate a line of stock, knowing that, because of these options, there will not be any large blocks offered for sale the moment the stock becomes active.

The officials of the company are interested in our plans, inasmuch as an active market for their company's stock is favorable to their business and to their stockholders. They, therefore, are pleased to cooperate with us by keeping us posted as to operations, increasing profits, and other pertinent details.

We call in a professional who has had a successful career as a pool manager, and retain him to act, first, as our purchasing agent and, second, as our salesmanager.

His first job will be to buy as cheaply as he can the amount of stock which we have decided to accumulate. He may do this by publishing conspicuously the statistics of the company's earnings, which during the past six months have been poor. He may then sell a quantity of stock "short," by which method he hopes to "bring out stock" from the public, thereby further depressing the price. Naturally, the time which he will select for this purchasing program will be when the market as a whole is weak technically and when public sentiment is pessimistic.

We having accumulated the stock, the important campaign remains. Our sales manager plans his advertising and publicity features. He releases information to the effect that business for the corporation is looking up. Statements from the president and treasurer are pre-arranged. Encouraging rumors are allowed to circulate. Financial statements are prepared for the press and for market-letter writers, brokers, and customers' men. Everything is planned ahead.

The most persuasive sales arguments, however, are rising prices for the stock. The principal medium used in this advertising plan is the ticker tape. In order to increase activity and interest, we may have to continue to buy stock for a while. Offerings from the rank and file of smaller traders will have to be absorbed; but they should not be large, and these sellers will return later as buyers when they see the stock gradually, but steadily, advance in price. If too much buying comes along our pool-manager may sell some stock in order to prevent a too rapid advance.

During all this time the various publicity stories are circulated. A widespread interest grows in the affairs of the corporation. People begin to ask their friends if they have noticed XYZ. Brokers receive inquiries. The advertising campaign is having its effect.

Still our sales manager has not been able to sell a great amount of our stock. He has been forced to support the stock as traders have taken profits. Some speculators, noting the advance, have sold the stock short; and this selling is being absorbed all along; quite gladly, however, inasmuch as those who are selling short now become potential buyers, can be counted upon to add their purchase orders later when their aid is needed. In fact, our pool manager has been happy to lend stock to the short sellers, and has engineered several reactionary maneuvers purposely to invite short selling. (Occasionally pools themselves sell short against balance, if they find it necessary to do so in order to control the market action of their stock.)

As the public becomes more and more interested in our merchandise, the sales manager's job becomes more difficult. He has the professional element to deal with as well now, which is more difficult to outsmart than are the members of group two.

Rumors now are allowed more circulation; the public is buying greedily, believing that an extra dividend, or a "melon" of some kind, is sure. The pool manager begins selling stock in earnest; the increased activity causes faster rallies, and consequently more severe reactions. Each advance, however, reaches above the previous high price; and the public soon is confident that the stock will advance another hundred points, that there is no limit to the possibilities.

A terrific churning of transactions is the result, as our manager sells thousands of shares, only to buy and sell again and again. The climax is near. Nearly three-fourths of our stock is sold. It is time for the big moment.

The next morning, newspapers all over the country carry the welcome news that the corporation's directors have declared a stock dividend. Public enthusiasm is boiling. Our sales manager unloads all of our unsold stock, and his job is finished!

Part of our tale remains to be told. The public now has the stock. Some of them sell, then others; there are no supporting buying orders. Professionals, sensing that "the news is out," sell quantities of stock short. The price declines swiftly as margins are called and more stock is sold. When it has declined to a level attractive to investors, important buying will come into the market, short sellers will cover their previous sales, the corporation's officials may buy some stock, and the swift reaction is halted as the public sells out.

The public loses—that is, the public speculators, who bought on rising prices and sold out during the decline. Many of them in this imaginary operation of ours doubtless followed the schedule formulated by the brokerage office wit who advised traders to "Buy on tips, and sell on dips." I have drawn out this illustration at length because, I assure you, similar operations are being planned and carried out every month. Unless we understand the campaigns which are engineered to interest us in buying stocks, how can we hope to time our own speculative commitments in order to go with the professionals and sell when they do?

It is said that stocks seldom rise of their own accord, that they will sag under their own weight unless they are pushed up. I believe this is true, for it is difficult to understand how any stock can remain active unless there is some motivating power behind it. One by one would traders take profits, or sell to get into some other commitment. Dying activity will not attract speculators. It is the persistent buying, and selling, which creates activity and demand. There are doubtless several pools, and many professional operators, all interested at the same time in some of our most active stocks.

In order to make money from speculation we must trade in the active stocks—those stocks in which the professionals operate. The winning combination for us as traders is a stock in which a pool is active, which has strong sponsorship and support from a bank or banks, and the earnings of which are known to be progressively on the increase. Then, our problem is in the timing of our commitments—when to buy and when to sell.

Let us reverse this picture for a moment. We have been looking behind the scenes. Standing out in front, and realizing the magnitude of the operations carried on back stage, is it any wonder that the public usually guesses wrong? The individual trader faces one of the most difficult tasks conceivable when he attempts to outguess the keenest minds on Wall Street, who are on the inside. The trader must not lose sight of the fact that the "insiders" are usually well fortified with capital and are able to stand losses when their judgment misses fire.

In liquidating markets, however, of the kind we had during the latter half of 1930, pools, big operators, all, suffer—except, naturally, those operators who transfer their plans to the "short side" of the market. Operations to advance prices are not attempted in weak, or bear, markets by shrewd professionals. Occasionally one may try "to buck the trend" for a momentary gain; but, inasmuch as operators must have someone to buy their stocks, they almost always plan their operations for a time when the general market is favorable, technically and fundamentally.

A general in war-time envelops all of his movements in secrecy in order to mystify the enemy; likewise, a financial general plans his tactics so that the public and the other operators are kept guessing. I shall have a great deal more to say about stock maneuvers when we get into the discussion of tape reading; but it will do no harm to interject here the statement that it is utterly useless for us on the outside, who buy and sell comparatively small blocks of stock, to conjecture upon what "they" are doing. We cannot know what the insiders intend to do, but we can see their orders on the tape when they execute them. That is why my plea is for every one of us to have no mere opinions of his own, but to allow the action of the market to tell him what is passing. We shall discuss this aspect of the subject more fully later on.

Do not be discouraged if you have lost money in the market. Nearly everyone did during 1929 and 1930. Many big traders lost everything and have had to start anew. Pools were forced to liquidate with losses; banks called loans right and left, and practically demanded liquidation.

If you cannot lose cheerfully, do not trade in the market! It is no business for the person who is easily discouraged. Countless losses must be accepted: the problem is to limit the losses. No one may ever hope to become so expert that he never takes a loss.

Start in a small way and be satisfied with reasonable profits. If you decide to experiment with the theories and ideas discussed in this book, trade at first in odd lots. Do not plunge or become overextended. This is worn-out advice, I know, but margin and capital worries warp your judgment and hamper your trading skill. When you think you have become familiar with technical action and can interpret market movements—and can take losses quickly—not until then should you speculate with larger lines of stocks. There is no disgrace in being a small trader, and the market will remain open for business for a good many years to come.

Another thing—the views of all of us were thrown out of perspective during the severe depression and market strain of 1929 and 1930. Many of our mental attitudes formed in those years may need adjustment in the months and years ahead. The main principles, as you will find them set down in this book, are, I believe, dependable; but our minds must be swung about to look at market conditions in a different light. We must attune our powers of perception to the period ahead, and not everlastingly compare every factor with some occurrence in the recent past.

New conditions will arise. A new trading public will be born. However, the old cycle of rallies and reactions will roll on. We shall have "over-bulled" movements and disastrous crashes. And the uninformed, unintelligent public will buy when security prices are high and sell when they are low. New traders will be seen in brokers' offices generously buying stocks at the wrong time from the "older heads" on Wall Street.

Manipulations and pool operations may require more capital to cope with a new and larger public, but the old methods will remain.

One last request and we shall turn the page and get into the subject of tape reading. If you are not willing to study, if you are not sufficiently interested to investigate and analyze the stock market yourself, then I beg of you to become an outright long-pull investor, to buy good stocks, and to hold on to them; for otherwise your chances of success as a trader will be nil.

PART TWO
TAPE READING

CHAPTER 2

THE TICKER TAPE

BEHIND THE TAPE

In Part One we have seen something of the power behind the ticker. You will agree with me, I am sure, that it will tax our ingenuity, observation, and perceptive judgment to the limit if we are to be successful in foretelling from market action when stocks will advance and when they will decline. (These discussions relate to the intermediate trends and minor fluctuations of stock prices, and not to the long-term, or commonly called "long-pull," trends.)

Market action—the buying and selling of stocks—is recorded on the tape. To the uninitiated eye and brain the tape means little—it is simply a confusion of hieroglyphics and figures. To the student, however, it offers opportunities commensurate with the skill, judgment, study, and self-mastery employed.

As the tape records money transactions, I am going to ask you to forget, for the time, the word "points" when discussing stock quotations and think instead in terms of dollars. The mention of dollars immediately conjures up the idea of buying and selling. For instance, if you notice a 5,000-share transaction of Steel (symbol, X) on the tape at $170, call to your mind the fact that this means that $850,000 worth of common-stock certificates of the United States Steel Corporation have changed hands. If you then notice, some hours later, another exchange of the same quantity at $175, realize that this, translated, means an increase in value of $25,000. To me such transactions take on a far greater significance if spoken of in terms of dollars than they would if someone said: "Steel advanced five points."

Before we attempt to understand the technicalities of tape reading, let us picture in our minds the scene behind the symbols. If you have never visited the New York Stock Exchange, I suggest you do so at your first opportunity. In the mean time, visualize a marketplace where hundreds of men are busily engaged in buying and selling goods. You see a little knot here in this corner where one man in the center has orders from his clients to buy, we will say, 1,000 shares of American Can stock at $150 per share—an order totalling a value of $150,000; quite a sizable piece of business. The other men in the group may each have smaller orders to sell: one is willing to sell 300 shares; another, 200; and so on.

On the floor of the Exchange there are many groups such as the one described. These men spend their entire time between 10:00 and 3:00 o'clock each day executing orders which they receive from their offices—orders placed by you and me and the hundreds of thousands of buyers and sellers throughout the world. There are also floor traders—members of the Exchange—who buy and sell stocks for their own account. All of these orders for millions of shares of stocks are recorded on the tape.

In order to visualize the enormous amount of business which is transacted, let us take a day when a total of 4,000,000 shares was bought and sold. The average price of 300 active stocks on December 16, 1930, was $39.89. The volume of sales in these 300 stocks was 3,625,700 shares. This makes a total of $144,629,173 for this one day alone! You can easily imagine what the figure would have been eighteen months previous. These amounts are highly significant, as will be pointed out later, when we come to the discussion of the volume of transactions.

In the first part of this book I have described the various kinds of people comprising the purchasers and sellers of stocks. The important point to remember here is that all of these people are human beings, just as you and I are. Some are more experienced in the stock market than are we; many, less. Some are conservative; many are pure gamblers. Nevertheless, with the exception of the few who purchase stocks for income only, each person is interested in the same thing as you and I are: the profit to be realized from the transaction. We are motivated by the same desires and are affected by the same emotions (in varying degrees, of course, in accordance with our temperaments and training). In short, we are all human beings trying to make money by exercising our speculative, intuitive judgment; we are hoping to make our capital funds work for us at an exorbitant rate of return.

Let us get that picture clearly in mind. The ticker tape is simply a record of human nature passing in review. It is a record giving us the opinions and hopes of thousands of people. We must dismiss from our minds all other facts. Precious few know, or can hope to know, who is buying or selling. We hear that So-and-So is buying; he may also be selling, through another broker. If he wants us to know that he is buying, we should be chary. So, let us disregard hunches and wild conjectures. If he buys and sells, the record of his transactions will be on the tape. We must make our interpretation from the record. So long as we continue to guess who is doing the buying and selling, we shall remain in a sea of confusion.

The person who is privileged to know who is buying, does not need the ticker tape.

You will find more discussion in brokers' offices upon what "they" are doing in the market than you will find students who realize the futility of conjecturing upon something about which they can know nothing. We learn from the professional traders, pool operators, and the important banking groups, only what they wish to have known—do not forget that! Do not forget for an instant, either, that the invisible "they" are trying to accomplish exactly the same result that you and I are: to make profits from their commitments. The solution to the whole problem of speculation in stocks is to judge and foresee what the other fellow is doing. And, there is one thing more for us not to forget: we are pitting our brains against the sharpest mental equipment in the United States.

Is it any wonder that relatively few are able to earn money consistently from speculation?

Let me suggest one thought for your consideration. The insiders (see explanation in Part One) have the greatest advantage over us in the minor fluctuations. It is my opinion that there is little use in trying to make money consistently by trading in and out of stocks hourly, or daily. The longer the trend, the more opportunity we have to be right. This is why I urge always that trading be confined to the intermediate trends.

The Tape

Now let us look at the ticker tape itself.

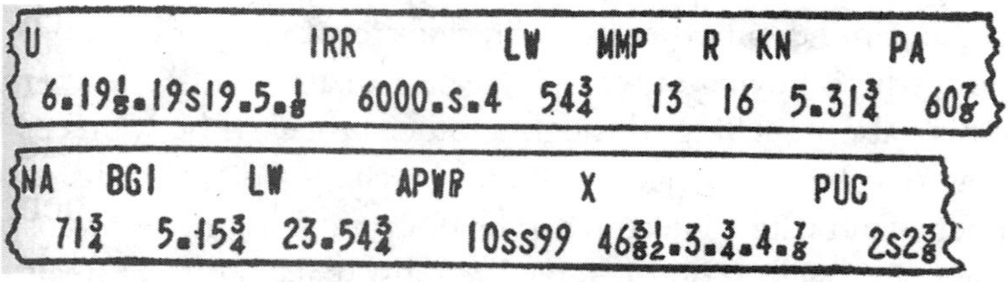

Plate 1

The letters are the symbols for the different stocks. Under the letters are figures, some broken by dots, or little black squares, and others by "s." The letter "s" and the dot mean the same thing: a division between the number of shares traded and the price at which the exchange has been made. Wherever "ss" appears, it is a record of an odd-lot transaction (one of less than 100 shares), which is reported on the tape for preferred stocks and common stocks whose unit of trading is less than 100 shares. The last two zeros are not printed in recording the volume of shares, unless the exchange is of 5,000 shares or more.

In "strings" of stock, very often the whole number is left off and only the fraction printed where it is readily apparent what price is meant; for example, in the string of United Corporation, U (see Plate 1), you will note that the last transaction in the string is simply given as "5.⅛," which means "500 shares at $19⅛." Likewise, in order to speed up the record on the tape the first figure of stocks selling over $100 is often left off when the price is quite familiar to traders. An example of this practice is to be found in the report on the string of United States Steel, X, where the $46⅜ shown actually means $146⅜.

Reading from left to right, the strips of tape illustrated will read, when translated, as follows:

United Corporation:
600 shares at $19⅛
1,900 "   " $19
500   " " $19⅛

Indian Refining:
6,000 shares at $ 4

Loew's:
100 shares at $54¾

Miami Copper:
100 shares at $13

Radio Corporation:
100 shares at $16

Kennecott Copper:
500 shares at $31¾

Pennsylvania Railroad:
100 shares at $60⅞

North American:
100 shares at $71¾

Briggs Manufacturing:
500 shares at $15¾

Loew's:
2,300 shares at $54¾
Atlas Powder, preferred stock:
10 shares at $99

United States Steel:
100 shares at $146⅜
100   "   " $146½
300   "   " $146¾
400   " $146⅞

Park Utah Mines:
200 shares at $2⅜

As you know, the unit of trading on the New York Stock Exchange is 100 shares, and sales of odd lots are not reported on the tape except for a few stocks whose unit of sale is 10 shares. This is really helpful to the tape reader, as he may base his opinions upon the transactions of buyers and sellers who have sufficient capital to trade in 100 or more shares. Of course, odd lots, grouped in larger units, make their appearance from time to time. This is valuable information. Naturally, you cannot determine whether a transaction for, let us say, 1,200 shares is made up of odd lots, or not; but you can see the result of the 1,200-share exchange.

What the Tape Shows

In all that I shall have to say, I warn you that I see on the tape only the results of buyers' and sellers' transactions in stocks; mine are not eyes that perceive the occult signs of movements of J. P. Morgan and Company or short sales executed by Jesse Livermore. Mr. Livermore may be buying, or selling; but if the stock advances, and I am "long," I shall be content. Inasmuch as I am not well acquainted with any member of J. P. Morgan and Company, or with Mr. Livermore, I am quite certain that they are not interested in me as an individual. However, they are interested in me collectively. Here is what I am driving at: the individual trader tries to find out what some important operator is doing, but he never stops to think that that operator must tell from the action of the stock he is operating in what the public, of which the individual trader is a member, is doing. It strikes me as a fair arrangement. The pool manager or major operator may have several millions of dollars at stake. If he is willing to pit his judgment against that of the public, we should be willing to risk our capital without expecting him to tell us personally what he is doing. If we wish to attempt to make easy money, we cannot complain of the risks.

While I agree that the movements of stocks often respond to the "pull on the strings" on Wall Street, I also know that our biggest operators have been fooled many times by the public. The year of 1930 will remain in these operators' minds for a long time. We have all heard of the blocks of stocks which had to be liquidated at disastrous prices. "They" take their losses; so must we. The man who buys and sells from 25 to 500 shares of stock, has little worry when it comes to selling; he always has a market. But, the operator "long" of thousands of shares often finds he cannot sell them.

Our problem, therefore, simmers down to this: how to judge, from the action as reported on the ticker tape, the future movements of those two composite human beings—the buyer, made up of all buyers, and the seller, made up of all sellers—whose transactions the tape pictures for us. The price tells us what the buyer is willing to pay for a stock and what the seller is willing to take for his shares. The volume (the number of shares per transaction) tells how much the buyer is able, and willing, to spend in backing up his judgment, and, conversely, how many shares the seller is willing to let go at the price offered.

CHAPTER 3

THE PRINCIPLES OF TAPE READING

TAPE INTERPRETATION

Tape interpretation depends upon a consideration of the action of the volume. It is not price action, but volume—the amount of money, the supply and the demand—which best tells the story. You will readily agree that it makes a great difference whether tile buyer is willing to pay $15,000 for 100 shares of Steel (X-150) or $150,000 for 1,000 shares (X-10.150). The demand is greater in the latter case, as is the supply. Do not forget that every purchase of a share of stock means a sale also. Our job is to determine the balance of the supply and the demand: whether the demand is greater than the supply, in which case the price advances, of course; or the reverse. The action of the volume tells us of the supply and demand; price merely denotes the value of the volume.

Tape reading is an art, rather than a science. After experience and familiarity with varying types of markets, the trader arrives at a stage where his intuition comes into play. He then has the "feel" of the tape. I cannot hope to pass along this intuitive understanding of tape reading; but if you understand the principles and hints herein pointed out, not many months should pass before you begin to get this "feel." Familiarity with many symbols, a quick eye, concentrated observation of important transactions, or the lack of them, and a studied belief that the philosophy and psychology of the tape are the all-important factors, will bring success—success in interpreting movements of prices, although not necessarily success in making money.

The latter will depend upon your own actions and reactions, your emotions, your ability to act in accordance with your opinions, and the hundred and one other human factors, many of which are to be discussed in Part Three of this book.

Do not be discouraged. If it were easy, there would not be any stock market; if it were not for the variance of opinions, active speculation would not exist and orders would be transacted over the counter.

GENERAL PRINCIPLES

For the sake of simplifying our problem, I shall here roughly define the three main types of volume activity:

First: Increasing volume during an advance, with the intervening pauses or setbacks occurring on light volume. This is indicative of the underlying demand's being greater than the supply, and favors a resumption of the advance.

Second: Increased volume at the top of a rally, or of an advance, lasting for some time, with no appreciable gain in prices—an active churning of stock transactions without progress. This is indicative of a turning point.

Third: A "tired," or struggling, advance, when stocks creep upward on light volume and "die" at the top. This indicates a lack of demand (few buying orders); and, whereas selling orders likewise are light, this action frequently marks a "rounding-over" turn, which may be followed by increased volume on the down side (when the sellers see that they cannot hope for much higher prices at that time). These struggling trends are subject to sudden reversals, particularly when they have endured for several days.

These types of action are present, but reversed in sequence, in declining markets.

I shall try to show in various illustrations how these principles work out. In some instances I shall refer to the larger movements, and to the main turning points of major trends, while in others I shall hope to demonstrate how the same action, in proportionately smaller units and in shorter spaces of time, gives the same indications. Broadly examined, the principles are found to be the same, whether employed within one day's range for a forecasting of the subsequent minor fluctuations, or during and following an intermediate or a major trend.

CHAPTER 4
INCREASING VOLUME DURING AN ADVANCE

I have stated that the essence of tape reading is the interpreting of the action of the volume. The broadest example of this is when the market rallies briskly, with the volume of transactions increasing—millions of dollars' worth of stocks changing hands. After a time, it will be noticed, stocks generally slow up in their advance. Right then is the important time to watch the volume. If the volume decreases perceptibly with the diminishing advance of prices, it is a favorable sign, indicating that, although purchasing orders have slowed down, there is not a heavy supply of stock offered for sale; otherwise, an immediate reaction would set in. If, following this stabilizing period, prices begin to decline, watch for increasing volume on the downward path. If prices sag under slight pressure—that is, if the volume of transactions is dull, in hundreds of shares rather than in large blocks—it is again a favorable signal for the resumption of the advance later. It is from this action that one of the old adages of Wall Street doubtless sprung: "Never sell a dull market." I believe that this was intended for bull markets, for it appears just as dangerous to "buy a dull market"—during a bear market.

Therefore, watch for dullness to appear on reactions, for then you may expect a resumption of the advance. Conversely, small volume on rallies, after a decline, is an indication of lower prices later. During the summer and fall of 1930, when stock prices were declining disastrously, the rallies were marked by an immediate lessening in the volume of transactions: volume dried up on rallies. During the declines, however, volume increased rapidly. It simply meant that there was a far greater amount of stock for sale than the buyer would purchase, except at constantly cheaper prices.

Chapter 5

Turning Points on Heavy Volume

Heavy Volume But No Headway

Heavy volume at the end of a move is extremely important, inasmuch as it generally indicates a turning point in the market. In this situation, on the upward side, we have volume during the advance with continued, increasing activity of transactions at the top without stocks making further headway. In other words, our buyer wants more stock and continues to enter order after order; meanwhile, our seller, who previously would sell only on advancing prices, now offers for sale great quantities of stock. For a time there is a tug of minds between buyers and sellers, but this extreme activity near and at the top is indicative of a substantial reaction to follow.

This is true, likewise, at the bottom. You are familiar with some of the turning points of the declines in 1929 and 1930, when volume increased tremendously. June 18, 1930, furnished an example. On that day more than 6,000,000 shares changed hands. Late in the day a rally set in, and soon buyers were bidding for stocks, whereas just before that all the weight was on the side offering stock for sale. There were many of these volume days during 1929 and 1930. September and October, 1929, witnessed this churning of stocks at the top.

Lesser movements are marked by the same characteristics. I have mentioned these big days because the illustration is clearer.

Let us run over these first two phases of volume action and translate them into terms of human action.

Volume Indicating an Advance

During the rally, what has been going on? Two things: first, the buying of stocks by those who are covering their previous short sales; and, second, new buying by those who expect the advance to continue. Both factions are spending their money to purchase something; but one faction is closing out a transaction, while the other is entering one. The man who covers his short position is in a greater hurry than the long buyer. The short seller will rush to cover if he believes that the rally will endure for some time. If you are contemplating a purchase (likewise, if you consider selling stock which you own), you are interested in both of these opinions—the judgment of John Smith, who is short, and that of John Jones, who is buying stock to hold for the advance. You would like also to determine whether there are many more Smiths than Joneses—more short-coverers than long buyers—because if the rally is due mainly to short-covering it is likely to be brief, and may be followed by further declines.

How can you tell which it is? Watch the volume and, in this situation, the rapidity of price changes. If you are considering purchases, you will probably not be in a rush; and, furthermore, you will not wish to buy if you feel that an order "at the market" may be executed at two or three dollars per share more than you see on the tape. On the other hand, if you are short, and feel the decline has spent itself, you will place your buying-orders at the market, satisfied to get out with your profits.

Let us assume that you sensed the turn at the bottom and purchased two or three stocks. Your interest now would be to decide whether to hold for a sizable advance, or to throw out your stocks if you misjudged the turn in the trend. Your problem then resolves itself into determining whether good buying comes into the market along with short-covering. (By "good buying" is meant purchases made by those who are in a position to know the underlying conditions of the market, and also the buying done by those who are sponsors of certain issues.) You notice large blocks of stocks taken at steadily rising prices. At intervals, the market becomes quieter, with less volume and fewer transactions; yet you notice that coincidentally there is very little weakness apparent; that reactions are on transactions of only 100 to 1,000 or 2,000 shares: there are few huge blocks frequently changing hands at lower prices.

Stopping here just a moment, may I ask: "What would you do if you were still short? Or what would be your inclination if you were considering purchases?"

If you were short, I believe that the fact that the prices did not sag, that the market was firm, would make you think to yourself: "Here, I had better buy in my stocks while I still have profits," or "before my losses become larger." Likewise, if you wanted to purchase, but had not made up your mind, you might hesitate somewhat longer; but at the first signs of higher prices you would be likely to jump in with your orders.

In this imaginary market, let us assume that we have witnessed a swift rally which lasted for two hours. The dullness which has followed, with prices only a dollar or two under their "highs," has lasted another two hours or so. Opinions are evenly divided. Those who expect lower prices are selling, while others are cautiously buying. Soon you notice a block of 3,000 or 10,000 shares of your stock, or a transaction much larger than normal, change hands at the same price as that of the previous sale. Your mind becomes alert at once; you have been watching for just this signal. (Of course, this signal may have been a series of "strings" at gently advancing prices, or any unusual block.) Again, following the unusual transaction, there are other individual sales in your stock. At the same time, you notice volume trades in other stocks. Likewise, Steel is gaining in momentum.

Your attention now is riveted upon the tape in order to see at once whether these larger transactions following the dullness are going to confirm your expectations that the advance will be resumed. Before long you will know definitely. The market may pick up momentum, with our guide, volume, pointing the way; and higher prices may be recorded. Then, if you have not covered your short sales, you undoubtedly will. So will others, and another rally will be in the making. But this time, inasmuch as it is the second step, the buying will be more courageous, and the advance should continue for a longer period. (I might mention at this point that stocks frequently rally in three-day periods, and consequently their market action at the ends of these periods should be more carefully analyzed if you are attempting to catch the active movements of stock prices.)

In the event that the unexpected happens, and volume increases at *lower* prices, it would be well to sell your trading holdings at once and stand aside. A further increase in volume in the downward direction will wipe out the rally, and we are back where we started from. In the majority of situations, however, dullness following the rally indicates resumption of the advance. But *do not argue with the tape*. Find out whether the buyer is stronger than the seller, or the opposite, and act accordingly. Volume will give you your answer.

DETECTING THE TURN OF A TREND

Now let us suppose that we see an active churning of stocks attended by heavy volume, but without appreciable price headway made. This, as we know, is indicative of a reversal of the trend. During this period, whose length depends upon the importance of the turn, some stocks may soar into new highs (or may make new lows, if the *downward* trend is about to be reversed), but the majority are simply traded in heavily without gaining or losing ground. This character of action is often caused by the professionals' bidding up market leaders in order to liquidate other stocks. It is a good plan at this juncture, if a major turning point is imminent, to study the action of the second- and third-rate stocks. They may give you early confirmation of the reversal. For example, in 1929 the inactive stocks began their decline some weeks ahead of the market leaders. At that time, public speculation was so rampant that buying-power was not dissipated for weeks. The high day for the market averages was September 2, yet leading stocks did not break into their definite downward trend until the middle of October.

Within the lesser movements of prices we have these same characteristics. The market, in normal periods, is continually rallying and reacting within the major trend. During the summer and fall of 1930, there were many rallies and reactions; the trend however, was down. Nevertheless, the same principles which I have described hold true for the intervening movements.

Translated into human terms, the causes are simple enough. The prices of stocks are nothing more than the decisions of all buyers and sellers of stocks. At turning points, the opinions—whence come decisions—are evenly divided. Buyers and sellers, both, are busy.

Let us go back just a moment to the action preceding a top turning point. The public is attracted by price changes, not by volume; that is to say, the public does not analyze the action of volume. It is prior to and during these final stages of a move that the professionals and pools unload their stocks on the inexperienced. The unwary, having seen prices advance steadily with only minor set-backs, misinterpret the feverish activity and buy heavily—which is just what the professionals want. In fact, pool managers operate upon this human weakness and engineer rapid run-ups of prices, knowing that thousands of traders and buyers will be attracted by this activity. Volume increases tremendously at these points, and newspapers carry front-page stories.

Not only are the final stages of a long trend, when prices do not materially advance, indicative of a turn, but also is the rapid action of prices with heavy volume, prior to the top, a danger signal. These periods together are referred to on Wall Street as the "distributive area," although the distributive area, strictly speaking, consumes a longer period of time, inasmuch as pools will distribute stocks during the latter part of the way up and part of the way down, after the top has been formed.

Various Turning Points

Many factors must be taken into consideration when we are interpreting the volume of turning trends. For example, the volume on June 18, 1930, which marked the approximate bottom of a severe decline, was 6,000,000 shares. At the end of the decline in August, 1930, owing to the decrease in the number of active margin-accounts, the selling climax came with only 3,400,000 shares traded. I well remember that day, because I was short of the market, and was trying to decide whether there was sufficient volume to mark the turning point or whether the selling was likely to carry much farther. However, the action had many of the ear-marks of a "clean-out," of a temporarily oversold condition. Although there was a terrific churning of stocks, little headway was made for approximately three hours. There was no progress on heavy volume. That was our signal.

However, when the market temporarily reversed its trend later in the year, in November, following a decline which had continued steadily for fifty-one days, we did not have the big volume day. Why? Because margin accounts with brokers were at the minimum; brokers' loans were down to the lowest on record. Actual liquidation had gone on for weeks. Liquidation from strongboxes and necessitous selling by large interests are not dumped upon the market as are stocks held on margin by the public. (The *speed* of the crashes in the fall of 1929 was caused by this panicky dumping of margined stock.) Therefore it was necessary to estimate the extent of liquidation already accomplished and to wait for the signs of the turn.

It was a difficult period; and I admit that twice I "felt for the bottom" with orders, only to learn soon that I had misjudged the action. Fortunately, it is not often that we witness liquidating markets; and we must be watchful not to train our "tape sense" on abnormal action.

At least a temporary turn came on November 10, and the signal was reasonably clear; but this time I found it necessary to turn almost wholly to the human side of the market for the clue. We all know that the public usually is wrong. Not being able to tell from the tape whether the end of that particular period of declining prices had come, I visited several brokerage offices and talked with managers. I found that their board-rooms were suddenly crowded once more. More important, I learned that nearly everyone wanted to sell short. I felt the time had come for a turn; and, sure enough, the next day the market started a substantial rally. Of this information of the public's action I found confirmation on the tape. There were signs of an oversold condition; and one more experienced than I in reading tape action, doubtless would have seen them without turning to examine other factors, as I felt it necessary to do.

I have brought in these personal experiences only to point out the various factors present. In the foregoing I have discussed tape reading mostly from the standpoint of the market as a whole, but later I shall include examples dealing with individual stocks.

Chapter 6

Turning Points on Light Volume

The Struggling Market

The characteristics of a struggling market are: a slow or irregular advance of prices, light volume, and dullness in general. (Reverse the illustration for the turning point after a struggling decline.)

If we are holding stocks for an advance, action of this kind tries our patience—which is exactly what it does to the other hundreds or thousands who are waiting for profits. No one seems willing to bid for stocks in any quantity; yet there are few sellers offering blocks of stock, realizing as they do that the demand is not sufficient to absorb them.

What is the natural outcome? Either one of two results, and the action of the volume should tell us which it is. The buying may eventually dry up, and the selling increase, as sellers see that they cannot hope to dispose of their stocks at higher prices. This may bring on an abrupt downward trend, the indications of which will be the appearance of larger blocks of stock offered at continually lower figures. (See Plate 2 and following text for explanations.)

The second eventuality is that prices will roll over and sag under their own weight, without the increase of selling pressure. In other words, the market struggles up and turns over as impatient holders take profits, or sell out in disgust. While the demand dries up, the supply likewise remains light. We then have a sagging, dull reaction, following the tired upward movement. This may continue until a level is reached where there is a greater demand, which, in turn, will be indicated by larger blocks. These dull markets may reflect a temporary indecision of the speculative powers, who await definite news from the business world. They may follow a severe upset, when public sentiment is at a low ebb and the professionals simply "sit tight" until the public "forgets."

These markets are difficult to follow because you can tell neither whether they will roll over on light volume nor whether they will be reversed suddenly. The latter is the more frequent; and for that reason the trader is doing the wise thing to step aside, or to protect himself against large loss by placing stop-loss orders against his commitments.

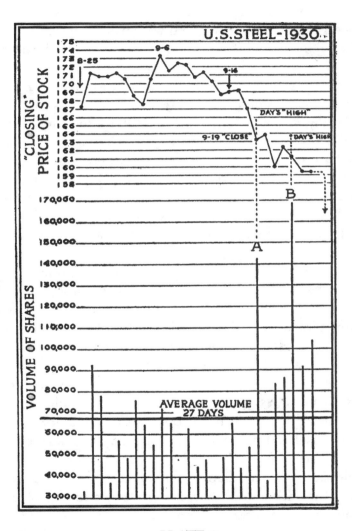

PLATE 2

A Sluggish Top

The action of Steel at the top of the September, 1930, rally, is a good example of the rolling-over top, followed by a pick-up in volume on the down side.

As you will notice in Plate 2, Steel fluctuated listlessly for 20 days within a 6-point range, and was unable to make any progress on the up side. The action on the 16th and 17th was more significant on the tape than I can show here on the graph of daily closing prices; nevertheless, it was difficult to come to a definite opinion about its meaning one way or the other.

Finally, on the 19th (marked "A") volume suddenly increased to 142,000 shares, as contrasted with an average of only about one-third that amount in the three weeks previous. The action on the tape was conspicuous: steady offerings of stock in large volume, with no let-up during the declines. The occasional rest periods during the day were marked by dullness. The action at "B," likewise, was significant, in that important selling was again conspicuous, as at "A."

A study of the broad top will explain the theories of struggling markets. You will notice a distinct diminishing trend in the volume (represented by the vertical lines at the bottom) during the formation of the top. In other words, in this particular example we witness drying-up of volume at the top—indicative of a turn—and the confirmatory action in the increased activity on the reaction. As mentioned in the previous description of struggling markets, occasionally these periods of dullness are followed by aimless, quiet fluctuations both up and down, which, in turn, result in firm stabilization, and then are followed by further advances. However, even in these instances, if we await the confirmatory action following the dullness, we shall detect our signal. The trader, meanwhile, loses little by standing aside until he satisfies himself of the outcome. The action of Steel in January and March, 1930, will illustrate this. See Chapter 15, pages 94 to 98, and Plates 15 and 16.

TOPS MORE DIFFICULT TO DISTINGUISH THAN BOTTOMS

Top-signals of the market as a whole, or of the market averages, are not as readily discernible as bottom-signals. The reason for the difference in action is that, in making for a top, all stocks do not reach their pinnacles at the same time, because, broadly speaking, buying is always, in any market, more slowly actuated than selling; whereas, in making for a bottom, stocks gain momentum as prices decline, and the rank and file, becoming panicky, dump stocks without rhyme or reason, and thus bring on a climax.

We have many rounding-over tops of the general market, as differentiated from sharply defined bottoms. The best illustration of this is the broad two to three months' top in the fall of 1929, as contrasted with the bottoms in the single days of October 29 and November 13, 1929.

In detecting the tops of moves, therefore, we must watch our individual stocks and not depend upon the general market for the signal to sell. However, when we notice that the market as a whole, as reflected in stock averages, slows up—becomes tired, and is apparently struggling to make higher peaks—we then are safe in assuming that the demand is not sufficient to push stocks farther without an intervening reaction. That is the time to analyze with particular concentration the action of individual stocks, because volume as a signal of the composite market is often deceiving, inasmuch as the top may consume several days and, therefore, each day will not be marked by conspicuous volume.

These tired-appearing markets must be carefully analyzed, as I have said, because in straightaway bull markets this action sometimes becomes nothing more than a rest-period (see page 92-93 and Plates 15 and 16), after which the advance is resumed. You will notice, however, from the following examples, that when tops are formed we do get the signal from volume—either at the top, followed by an immediate "turn-over" on greatly increased volume, or with a slowly "falling-over" top followed by the momentous volume a day or more later. Thus it may be broadly stated, that markedly increased volume following a run-up in price signifies distribution.

A Sharply Defined Top

In Plate 3 is shown the July, 1930, top in American and Foreign Power. It hardly needs explanation. The three-day spurt to the top was followed by a sudden turn-over on the 30th from a high of 77 to a closing price of 73, attended by heavy volume. You will notice in this illustration that the high figure of the top day exceeded that of the day previous by only $0.25 per share; yet the volume at this last drive was larger. (The curve in the chart, by the way, is formed by the high prices of each day.) The period covered is from July 14 to August 10, 1930.

This is a clear illustration of how a stock oftentimes rushes up accompanied by heavy volume and turns over on a big volume day.

A Broad Top

The action of General Electric (Plate 4) at this time in July was not so simple to interpret. There was no clear-cut indication of which was the top-day, as there was in American and Foreign Power.

From an analysis of a full day's activity, you will see it was not until the 30th that we received a definite message that the supply exceeded the demand and that a top had been formed.

From the tape, however, we had earlier information. On the 16th there was terrific hammering between 69⅛ and 70½, with supporting orders withstanding the selling-drive. Ninety thousand of the day's total of 98,000 shares were exchanged during this tussle between buyers and sellers. At about 2:30 o'clock the selling pressure subsided, and GL ran up to close at 71⅝. The significance of this day's action is not discernible from the chart, which shows only the highest price for each day.

On the 18th the combat was resumed, but the outcome was reversed. There were only 28,700 shares traded during the first four hours, but between 2:00 and 3:00 o'clock the volume was 60,500 shares; yet the buyers were overpowered. No substantial progress was made on the advance. It was evident from the action of the volume that distribution was in process—that the selling in General Electric was better than the buying.

The 28th, the high day, was marked by persistent volume within a narrow range of one and a half points. Although General Electric had advanced sharply on light volume the day before, the offerings were extremely heavy on the 28th; and, while the demand was sufficient to absorb the selling waves for a time, it was plain to see that the supply of stock was greater. There were large blocks offered repeatedly each time GL advanced above 73. Finally, in the last hour, the tide definitely turned and the stock slumped quickly from 74⅛ to close at 73.

On the 30th, the selling was constant and persistent; there was no question that selling pressure far exceeded the demand. There was not a rally of consequence during the whole day—volume dried up each time liquidation slackened.

AMERICAN CAN'S JULY, 1930, TOP

I believe that one more illustration of top-action may be helpful. For this example, in American Can, I have had a chart prepared for the four days of July 26 (Saturday), 28, 29, and 30, 1930 (Plate 5). In order to show the action in finer detail than a day's unit, I have divided the days roughly into half-hour periods. The vertical lines at the top of the graph are the high and low ranges within these periods; the dots to the left of the lines are opening prices, and those to the right are closing figures. The deeper verticals at the bottom are volume indicators, under which I have marked the total volume and the number of transactions for each day.

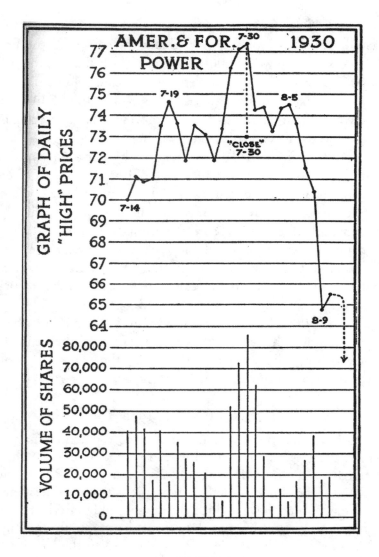

PLATE 3

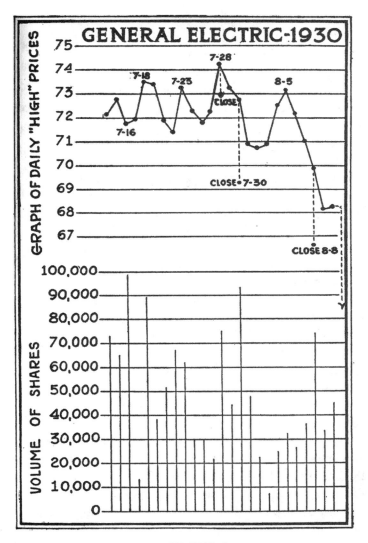

PLATE 4

41

At the first broad glance, you will at once see the volume day to have been the 30th, with prices declining steadily, and both the momentum and volume picking up as still lower prices were reached. There were 220 transactions on that day, practically double the number on the top-days; and the volume likewise was nearly twice as large. This action was apparent from the beginning, inasmuch as Can opened $1.25 per share higher than its previous closing, only to meet stock for sale and to turn down within less than an hour.

Now let us look at the previous days. Of course, if we had the tape running before our eyes, and could note the individual transactions and the strings of stock, it would be easier to put our fingers on possible important trades. However, it is reasonably clear from the chart. On Saturday, the 26th, the action was favorable for higher prices. Volume was large on the advances and light on the set-backs. Monday, however, told a different story. Soon after the opening, active buying sent Can across 134; and the reaction of about two dollars which followed was on less activity. Again it retraced its path and nearly reached 135. This time, however, the demand was less in evidence. After one more set-back, buying came on the tape quite conspicuously; and several times AC hammered at 135, and finally went through, but only for an instant. The action was significant in that the resistance at from 134 ½ to 135 was too strong, for that day, at least. In the appended chart (at "A"), which is drawn solely from transactions of 1,000 shares or more, you will see the large block of 3,300 shares which was offered at 135. There were several other 1,000 share lots offered earlier at just under 135.

On the 29th, Can opened $1.00 under the closing price of the night before, which indicated thin bids—light demand. Buying soon was uncovered, however, and the stock advanced again above 134½, only to have the demand fall off once more. The reaction which followed was, at first, not impressively heavy, although there were indications of increasing volume, which became quite evident later in the afternoon when activity picked up appreciably. Support came into the market in large blocks at 132, 132¼, and 132½; and this was sufficient to register a better closing price.

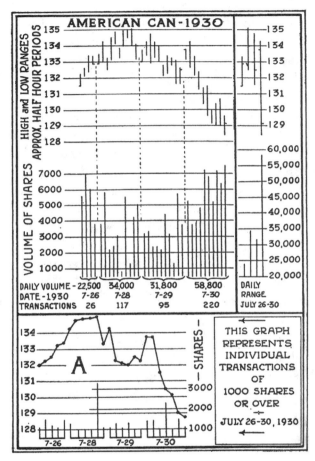

PLATE 5

We have discussed the action of the 30th. The selling pressure was apparent; our volume signals were there. Can appeared on the tape frequently, and more than a temporary reaction was plainly indicated.

This illustration, together with the example of General Electric and that of United States Steel (Plate 2), demonstrates that if we miss gauging the top-day—which is often difficult—we do soon have definite indications that a top has been formed. At the tape we can detect a resistance to the advance which is not apparent from the undetailed action of the day or from our evening newspaper quotations. Inasmuch as the wise trader will not attempt to sell at the top eighth, I believe that these illustrations will give some idea of the various types of action witnessed at tops, as well as an idea of the divers selling-signals. No two are ever alike; but, in the main, the chief characteristics prevail, and I think you will find that tops are formed by action which is recognizable under one of the three principles listed on pages 20 and 21.

These examples clearly demonstrate the necessity for concentrated analysis of the action of the market, in order to differentiate between the action of volume with no progress in price (buyers' and sellers' impasse), volume *during* a movement of prices, and dull, drying-up action.

CHAPTER 8

THE TAPE STORY OF LOEW'S

A DAY-BY-DAY ILLUSTRATION

A detailed tape story of Loew's action during November, 1930, will, I believe, be helpful, corroborating as it does, so completely, the principles of tape reading.

At least this action was of peculiar interest to me at the time, for I then owned the stock and, in consequence, for a while found myself quite uncomfortable.

In November, 1930, Loew's Incorporated, reported earnings for the year ending the preceding August 31 of $9.65 per share, which indicated a splendid record. On Plate 6, which gives the course of Loew's during the period from November 1 to December 2, you will note that this stock held up against the drastic selling waves common in the market at that time.

A PUZZLING REACTION

On November 5, 6, and 7 ("A" on Plate 6), the tape action of Loew's was not satisfactory. A trader watching the tape on the 7th would have seen the activity of volume in Loew's to be more impressive on the declines than on the rallies. In other words, the selling was better than the buying. One attempting to catch the minor intermediate fluctuations would have immediately sold his stock. There were plenty of opportunities to sell, inasmuch as the stock ran up well on light volume on several distinct occasions.

On November 12 ("B" on the chart), under increasing volume, Loew's dipped as low as 53¼, although it was able to close the day at 56¼. The volume of transactions on that day was 61,300 shares, as contrasted with an average daily turnover the week previous of about half that amount of stock. On November 13, Loew's opened at 56⅝, but sank steadily through the day until it reached a low of 53⅜. The next day it opened at 54¼, ran up to a high for the day of 55¾, and then under constant pressure of liquidation the stock, fell as low as 52⅝.

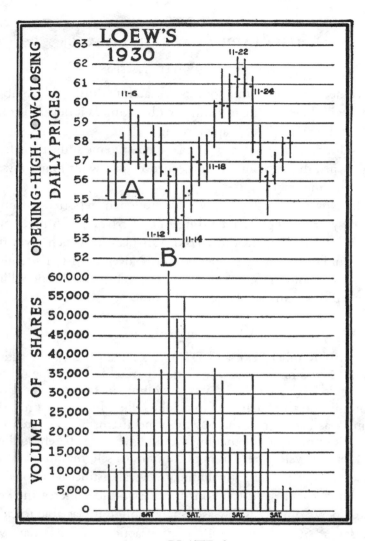

PLATE 6

It was at this point that there were numerous stories circulated, giving the reasons why the stock should go much lower. Three stories which were told to me as coming from "absolutely reliable sources," are instructive here as samples of market information, demonstrating as they do that the news we usually hear about a stock is already past history and probably untrue. I might well have been interested in these stories, but tried to practice what I am preaching here, and watched the tape off and on during the day for a reflection of the facts.

One man told me that owing to accounting, the earnings report of Loew's was inaccurate; and another, that the Shuberts were selling a large block of stock. The third story had to do with some tie-up with the Fox interests, who were forced to liquidate their Loew's holdings. If you have been in this same predicament yourself you will readily recall, no doubt, the effect such information has had upon you. However, I realized that these stories appeared after the stock had dropped some six or eight points (against the then *rallying* trend of the general market); and in watching the action of the stock on the tape I was convinced that the worst had already happened, because, when the stock was down to 52⅝ under swelling volume, the buying certainly appeared better than the selling. The stock declined but $0.75 per share below the figure of the previous day, under the largest day's volume but one in several weeks. This is a particularly good example, I believe, of "heavy volume without progress" marking the turn. This was confirmed later in the same day when the stock closed at 55¼, a gain of $1.25 per share above the previous day's closing price, and a recovery of $2.62½ from its low price on this turn-up day.

My reasoning in this situation was that the depression in the stock when the rest of the market started to rally, must have been due to some temporary situation. I have no doubt that one of the three stories mentioned may have had a basis in fact, but the trouble is that such stories are often circulated in order to assist those who have something to be gained. An active trader would have *purchased* Loew's on November 14 because of the action of the volume.

Perhaps it would be interesting if I followed through with this particular stock to show how the action on the following day, Saturday, further confirmed the action of the 14th.

The Action of Loew's on Saturday, November 15

Loew's opened at 55½. The stock was quite inactive for the first 40 minutes or so of trading, until a large block of Loew's changed hands at 54¾. The sale was for 2,300 shares. This was soon followed by another transaction of 100 shares at 54⅞, which, in turn, was followed by several individual transactions at 54¾. Sales at 55 then came out upon the tape in increasing volume.

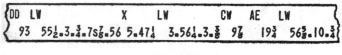

PLATE 7

Not long afterward, a string of Loew's appeared on the tape, as is shown in Plate 7: 100 shares at 55½, 300 at 55¾, 700 at 55⅞, and 100 at 56, immediately followed by 300 more shares at 56¼ and 300 at 56⅜. Almost at once there was another sale at 56⅝ and one of 1,000 shares at 56¾.

The important thing about these transactions was that, following upon the heels of the large block of 2,300 shares of Loew's at 54, the volume increased with the advancing prices.

Two more strings came out upon the tape, as is shown in Plate 8, one starting at 56⅞ and running up to 57¼ on 700 shares, and the other running up to 57⅝ on a volume of 1,000 shares.

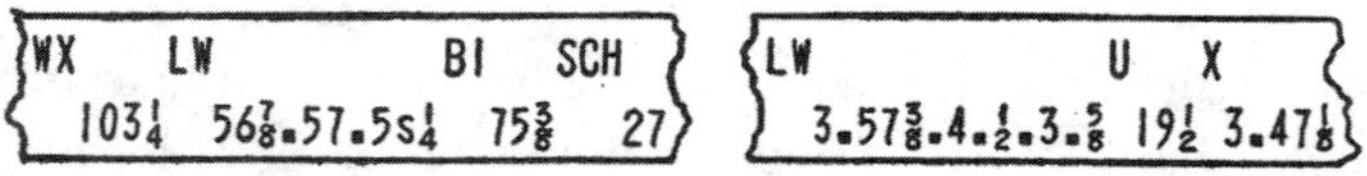

PLATE 8

The stock then became quiet, the volume receded, and there were several individual sales of 100 and 200 shares between 57⅝ and 56½.

Soon, however, 1,000 shares of Loew's changed hands at 57, only to be followed by another transaction of 100 shares at 57⅛, which, in turn, was followed by 100 shares at 57¼, 400 shares at 57⅜, 500 shares at 57⅝, and 600 shares at 57¾. (Incidentally, this type of action often takes place when important interests give an order to take all offerings up to a certain limit.)

Again there was a slight set-back on small volume, with a reaction to 56¾. Just before the close on Saturday, at about a quarter to twelve, there was slightly increasing volume. Then a short string of stocks came out with a good deal of volume, starting at 400 shares at 57½ and 2,100 shares at 57⅝. The stock closed the day strong at 57¼. The volume for the short two-hour session was heavy—29,700 shares: volume *during* the advance.

At about 12:00 o'clock the Dow Jones ticker reported the following: "Loew's—sharp recovery partly reflected completion of liquidation of a large speculative account in the stock," which is a further example of the truism that news is usually published so late that it is useless market-wise.

A favorable sign concerning Loew's during the morning was its lack of activity (no great amount of stock offered for sale) *following* the *active* run-ups.

This action of Loew's on this particular day is an illustration of one principle of tape reading. It is a favorable sign for a further advance if, after a run-up in a stock on reasonably heavy volume, the subsequent set-back occurs on light volume; in other words, if the volume dries up on the reaction.

The Action of Loew's on Monday, November 17

In order to continue the story of the action of this particular stock, I kept track of every transaction of Loew's on Monday, the 17th, and had a chart drawn of the day's action, including volume (Plate 9). You will notice that the interesting facts of this day's action were the increases in volume during the advances and at the tops of the day, and the one large transaction of 1,000 shares at 56⅝. You will remember that Loew's closed on Saturday at 57¼. It opened Monday at 57, and on the first three transactions of only 100 shares each the stock reacted to 55¾. Almost immediately, however, a rather steady advance set in with the volume increasing, but between 57 and 58¼ Loew's met quite a large amount of stock which was for sale. The action thus far was favorable inasmuch as the first advance was on increasing volume, but momentarily unfavorable in that the amount of stock offered for sale, and the number of transactions under greater volume on the 58 level, indicated that the stock would have a temporary set-back (volume without progress).

After this occurred, as you will note, the stock again sagged to 57⅛, while the volume diminished perceptibly. Loew's again ran up to 58¼, where more large blocks were offered, and again reacted quickly, only to rebound to 58¼ a third time. It was quite evident that the stock would have some trouble in getting through this 58-58¼ level, and after the third attempt the stock sold off for the remainder of the day. The 1,000 share transaction which suddenly appeared at 56⅝ was difficult to interpret, although it may well have been a buyer bidding for that quantity of stock which he had offered and sold short earlier in the day at the 58 level.

During this particular day, the volume on top of the advances was heavier than during the declines, from which it was apparent that some patience might be required before Loew's would be able to puncture the evident resistance level around 58.

Monday's action, shown in Plate 9, favored a subsequent advance. As more and more stock was absorbed at the 58 level, and so long as volume activity did not increase on the reactions, the tape reader would normally expect that the stock would have less difficulty in getting through this level later, inasmuch as there would be less stock offered for sale.

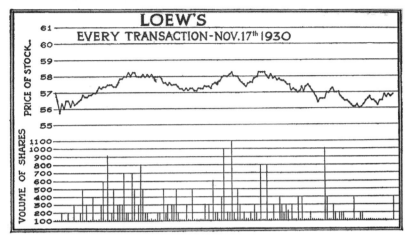

PLATE 9

THE ACTION OF LOEW'S ON TUESDAY, NOVEMBER 18

I shall not go into the details for November 18; but the action was quite confirmative, the stock again being active on advances and closing the day at 58, a gain of $1.12½ (1⅛ points) per share over the closing price of the previous day.

LOEW'S GOES THROUGH

In order to cut this story short I shall cover the next few days quickly. The stock advanced actively on volume on the 19th and 20th. The general market by the 21st had perceptibly slowed up in its advance, and Loew's, having regained its lost ground, also quieted down as it approached the 61-63 level. The volume dropped, as you will notice on the chart (Plate 6). My personal opinion concerning this tired action was that Loew's advance from 52⅝ to 62⅜ in only eight days was about all that could be expected for a while. I happened, fortunately, to select Saturday, the 22nd, to get out; chiefly because, as I judged from the tape-action, the "going was rough" on all attempted advances. On the 24th you will notice the pick-up in volume on the down side (35,000 shares for the day), which confirmed the lack of active demand during the days immediately before.

CHAPTER 9

STEEL, THE MARKET LEADER

WATCH STEEL

There is a saying: "As Steel goes, so goes the market." There is no question that X is the market leader, its bellwether. American Can, General Electric, Westinghouse, American Telephone, and a few other stocks, are also termed market leaders. They are, but the market will follow Steel when every other stock loses its leadership. This was particularly well illustrated, I think, in October, 1930, during the period of persistent liquidation. For days, American Can did not break; it held like a rock. Steel, however, led the market in the decline, or at least sagged simultaneously. I believe that if Steel had withstood the pressure, the market would have halted its drift likewise.

By the way, when you hear loose talk about "support-orders" in Steel, Can, and other leaders—when you are told: "They are going to support the market"—take out your pencil, add up the volume of transactions, and figure the millions "they" would need in order to support the market. Think in the same way when you hear stories to the effect that "they are going to run Steel up ten points." I do not imply that Steel is not ever supported, or that powerful interests do not push Steel forward at times—for they do—but they do it when the market is technically set for the maneuver. There are no interests in Wall Street powerful enough to stem the tide of wholesale public liquidation (this was proved in October, 1929); nor have they enough money to run Steel up 10 points, when they know from the market's position that thousands upon thousands of shares of Steel would be offered for sale all the way up. It is simple enough to sit around a brokerage office and glibly spin yarns about the "big fellows." Forget it; if any of your informants knew them well enough to know what they were doing, they would not be sitting in a broker's office talking to you and me.

To return to Steel: watch Steel closely at all times. Pay the same attention to its action that you do to your own stock. Your stock will probably rally with the market, if your selection has been correct; it may follow the market, or advance ahead of it; but it should not go against the trend. (If it does, check your position quickly, because when the general list does not follow Steel it is quite likely that many stocks are being sold under cover of strength in Steel.) Steel is a particularly helpful indicator because it is always active, thousands of shares being traded daily; and it never swings wildly, its market usually moving by eighths of a point.

If you hold an inactive stock (which is not recommended for short-turn trading), and for some time there have been no transactions in that stock, yet in the meanwhile Steel has reacted two or three points, it is well to "quote" your stock (obtain the bid and offered prices from the floor through your orderclerk). This will give you your "market;" otherwise, you may be disappointed when you finally see a transaction some dollars away from the last sale. Of course, if Steel is advancing and you are long, you need not feel uneasy; but it is none the less a comfort to have the "quote."

If you intend to watch the tape constantly, it is good practice to obtain the market on Steel, the bid and offered prices, shortly after the opening. From these you can detect whether Steel is being bid for, or whether it is offered below the bid price. Let me explain: assume that the market on Steel at five minutes after 10 o'clock is 149¼ bid and 149½ asked. If you notice 3,000 shares of Steel pass soon after at 149¼, you know at once that someone has "hit the bid," that in this block of Steel the selling has been more urgent than the buying. If it happens the other way about, with the transaction at 149¾, you will know that someone is bidding for stock and is willing to pay more than the asked price.

Watch for False Moves

Often, you will see a large block pass at a price under the bid figure, only to be followed by smaller transactions at prices running up above the offered price. Watch carefully; it may be a move to bid up the stock in order to sell another large block. Naturally, the seller wants to get the best price possible, and will marshal his movements to "make a good trade" if he can. Of course, you may notice several lots of Steel purchased at prices under the figure at which the large block changed hands. Here, if the buyer wishes to accumulate more Steel, he will endeavor to make it appear that there is plenty of Steel for sale in order that he can buy in another block at not too great an advance in price. This same maneuver may, of course, take place in any other stock.

If you are not in the habit of sitting over the tape constantly, you can gauge the market in the same manner by asking for the market on Steel at the time you happen to be at your broker's, and then check the situation a few minutes thereafter.

I have used the word "offered" in place of the more usual "asked" of the phrase "bid and asked," because, to me, "offered" means that stock is "wanting to be sold," not that someone will sell if you bid his price. In other words, the whole problem is one of solving the condition of the supply and demand—or, of the offerings and demand. Analyzing the volume in relation to the bid and offered prices will give you the clue to the supply and demand.

Naturally, you can check your own stocks in the same manner. I have dwelt at length upon Steel inasmuch as this leader will give you the situation of the market as a whole. I am assuming, of course, that you will glance around the board to see if there are any outstanding occurrences, and that you will ask your broker if anything exceptional has happened in your absence.

Incidentally, Steel is perhaps the most satisfactory trading stock on the board because it always has an active market.

THE ACTION OF STEEL IN AUGUST, 1930

In Plates 10 and 11 is shown every transaction in Steel for the days of August 12 and 13. This was the bottom of the market in August, 1930. Steel had been declining for 14 days, from 17 on July 28. I have marked the significant action on the 12th and

13th, "A" to "I." At "A" you will note the volume on the dips with dullness on the rallies. At "B" there was a distinct drying-up of activity at the day's tops, which lasted for several hours. Near the end of the day another reaction set in, with more volume; however, it met strong resistance between 157 and 157½, starting with the block of 2,100 shares. Volume was heavy during the day-end tussle ("C"), and for a few minutes it looked as if Steel were starting an advance out of the danger-zone. It "turned over" again quickly, but met an important block of 2,700 shares just before the close.

The following morning Steel was offered freely, and sank fractionally until a large order of 3,100 shares temporarily stopped its decline. At "D" there was another rally, but volume again was disappointing. The volume increased during the subsequent sell-off as far as "E," where important buying was again in evidence, which turned the tide finally. During the rally at "F" there was active bidding for stock, as the volume indicated. Although Steel did not advance far (only to 157¾), the reactions at "G" and at "H" were marked by shrinkages, instead of increases, in volume. The confirmation of the turn came at "I," when stock was well taken on steadily increasing prices.

Referring to the chart you will see that the real support came into the market on the morning of the 13th. The selling at "E" was important, as it was a test of the buying strength under the market. When very little stock was offered at "G" and "H," the trader would have stepped in with orders to buy. Of course, the whole market was acting similarly during this period. The market was oversold; but we did not have the sensational climax which we had had in May and June, and on other previous clean-out days, owing to the fact that there was a smaller number of the public selling, because so many had sold out, or had been forced out, before.

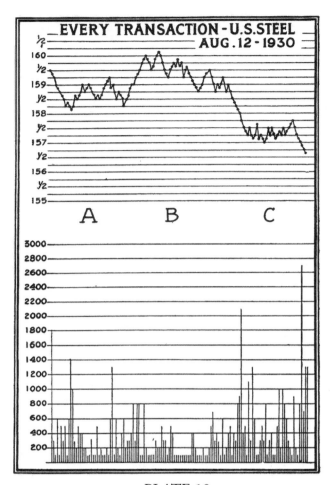

PLATE 10

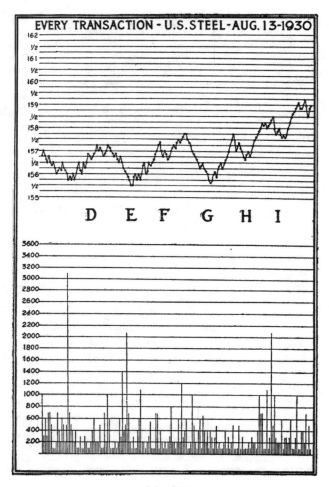

PLATE 11

A Word About the Examples in This Book

I realize that the reaction of some readers to many of the examples in this book will be: "It's easy enough to look at a chart of market action after it has passed and tell all about the signals, but it is a far different matter to foretell, as the action is taking place, what is going to happen." This is very true; but I believe that it will be recognized, as these illustrations are explained, that the principles do work out in practice. I shall have some suggestions to make further along for those who care to practice forecasting, but who cannot spare the time to watch every transaction on the tape.

I admit that only through practice can we acquire that "feel" which sends a definite signal to our brains when important action takes place. I cannot see, however, why we should expect to find a "system" which will work in the stock market; surely the possibilities of profits for the student justify the time and effort required to learn market interpretation. If there were a system, hundreds would have learned its secret; then it would not work, because too many would be using it.

Supply and demand: that is your guide; learn to recognize which is the stronger and you will make money trading. But do not expect always to judge correctly. Limit the losses caused by your mistakes and, when you are right, let your profits run. By this method you do not need many profits to offset several losses. You will readily perceive that a 10 or 12-point profit in, we will say, a 100 share trade, will offset several losses of two points each.

And *never overtrade*; maintain a margin of at least 50 percent.

CHAPTER 10
TIPS ARE DANGEROUS

CHECK YOUR TIPS ON THE TAPE

There is the greatest of danger in depending upon "contacts" and tips, as we know. Occasionally we receive information from someone in whom we have implicit confidence. Are we justified in committing ourselves blindly in the market upon such information? I say emphatically "No." But we can check up on this information, if we wish, by going to the tape.

Let me give you an example which was highly instructive to me. I have had charts drawn (Plates 12, 13, and 14 pages 61-65)) illustrating the movements of this tip.

In the latter part of September, 1930, an acquaintance of mine received information from the right source that certain interests were buying heavily in Electric Power and Light at around $63 per share. I cannot divulge further details, but ask you to take as true my assertion that the interests who were reported buying were certainly important. You will notice on the daily range graph (Plate 12) that there were signs of accumulation in the congestion that lasted over a period of several days. No one could quarrel with the accuracy of the tip at this juncture; but, tapewise, there were evidences later that offerings were becoming exceedingly heavy. The action of the volume gave the signal to sell, and to sell quickly. As you will notice, before I explain in detail the action of the stock, Electric Power and Light soon declined precipitously. My acquaintance was informed later that the avalanche of selling which had come into the market had been simply too great to absorb, and that, for this reason, "they" had had to step aside. Let us not forget this, in studying future markets: the strength of the public must not be underestimated.

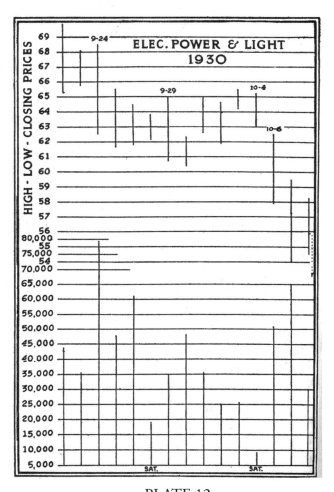

PLATE 12

The Action of Electric Power and Light

The action of EL will interest you, I believe, as it illustrates the accuracy of the principles I have set forth earlier. I shall discuss only the action during the week from Monday, September 29, to Monday, October 6.

On the 29th there was a good deal of selling, most of which occurred between 60¾ and 63 (Plate 13, which reproduces EL's action in *half-hourly* periods). Although prices gave way easily, there were signs of support, particularly in the manner in which the selling was absorbed near the end of the day, with the close at 61¼.

Tuesday, the 30th, was marked by much heavier volume than the day before, with many large blocks changing hands. As you will notice (Plate 13), prices made but little headway below the range of Monday. This staunch buying of the tremendous offerings was indicative of a turn, which came quickly the next day. This narrow-range day was difficult to analyze definitely, if considered alone; however, its significant characteristic was that during the entire active day no headway was made in either direction. On the only dip below the previous day ("A") the volume indicated strong support.

The stock opened Wednesday, October 1, $1.50 higher than at the close Tuesday. Selling orders were evidently withheld for the time. From this action on Wednesday one was justified in feeling that a sizable advance was pending: the stock appeared to act strictly in accordance with the tip. The following day, Thursday, the 2nd, the action was slightly disconcerting, in that prices slid off easily although the volume dropped down to a total for the day of only 25,100 shares. Inasmuch as the stock closed well above the day's low point we might have expected better prices the next day. One factor, however, was apparent, and that was that every time EL advanced to the 65 level it met stock for sale.

Friday morning's opening was indicative of the amount of offerings hanging over the market. The first transaction was 3,700

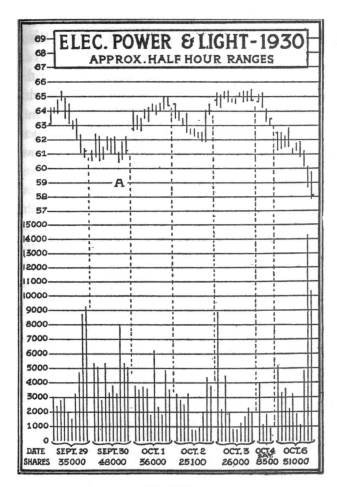

PLATE 13

shares, a $239,575 order. Soon, another large order of 2,200 shares was sold at 65, followed by several more good-sized trades around this same price. The day was marked by the evident danger from sellers whenever the 65 level was approached. We had at the top similar action to that which occurred lower down—fair volume without any progress. The slight rallies during Friday, the 3rd, were comparatively light in volume until the resistance level was reached, or punctured, when large offerings came upon the tape. I think a trader would have been warned by this action, at least to protect his trade with a stop-loss order at around 64, or else to sell out and stand aside for further definite indications.

We had those indications on Saturday, the 4th. Soon after the opening there was a large transaction of 3,100 shares at 65. Thereafter the stock sank steadily throughout the half-session, to close at 63½. There were occasional rallies, but whenever they occurred volume dried up immediately.

Monday was disastrous, as you will note from the chart (Plate 14), which shows every transaction, with volume. Bids were evidently light, as the stock opened $0.50 below the lowest point reached Saturday, on an initial order of only 600 shares. The selling during the first two hours ("A") was persistent, although no conspicuously large blocks were traded; rallies were dull, while the declines were in strings of quotations. Between 12 and 1:30 o'clock ("B") was a time of quiet before the storm which was to appear. The period starting a little after 1:30 witnessed the break, with volume during the last hour alone as great as it had been during the previous four hours. There was no let-up of consequence in the decline, except at greatly lessened volume. Here we had steadily decreasing prices with attendant large transactions—indicative of continued progress in the same direction.

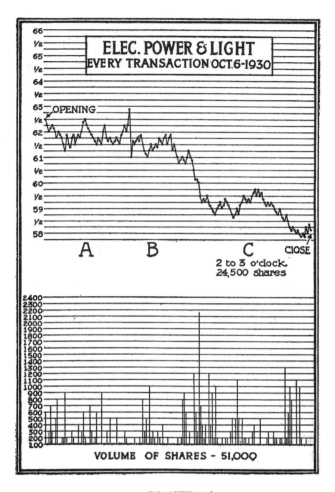

PLATE 14

65

So—Confirm It on the Tape

In these illustrations we have seen volume signalling turning points, defining resistance points, and marking substantial progress. It is particularly valuable, accentuating as it does the necessity and importance of having no opinions of our own unless they are confirmed by market action.

If we had purchased EL on the tip, the selling wave at the end of the day of the 6th certainly would have said: "Get out," if we had not taken the hint earlier from the fact that our stock ran into trouble upon every attempted advance.

Incidentally, from the chart standpoint alone (Plate 12), when EL broke through the congestion level on heavy volume, it was a definite signal to sell long holdings and go short. However, in this instance there were many individual signals which passed on the tape, but which are not discernible on a chart of the days' ranges. Also, our reliable signals came earlier on the tape.

CHAPTER 11

SOME IMPORTANT OBSERVATIONS ON VOLUME

VARIANCES IN VOLUME

I wonder if I have made myself clear when talking of "volume sales." I have sometimes stressed the importance of 5,000 share transactions, but in other examples have dwelt upon the importance of trades of only 1,000 shares. This importance of the *size* of the transaction depends upon the total activity. In other words, on some days stocks are traded much more actively than on others; there may be many more "volume-transactions" today than there were yesterday. I do not think, however, that that will give you any trouble, because you will sense immediately the *relative* importance of the varying sizes of blocks.

Bear in mind that 5,000 share transactions are printed in full and thus attract much more attention than a 3,000 or a 4,000 share trade, which is printed simply: 30.150 or 40.82½, as the case may be. Let the hangers-on notice and ejaculate about the fully printed orders; but you watch the sales of lesser volume also. You will then be able to attach a much more correct significance to the 5,000 share trade, because you will know whether it has followed several other important sales, or whether it is a signal which was flashed following a long period of dullness and inactivity. Bear in mind, also, that professionals know how much attention the 5,000 share transactions attract, and that they employ them for that very reason to trap the unwary.

Volume for the market as a whole is printed upon the tape at intervals during the day: at 10:30 A.M. and at 12:10, 1:30, and 2:10 P.M. From these figures of the volume you can judge whether your stock is normally or particularly active in comparison with previous days. You can also follow the market generally, and mentally note whether the market has picked up activity on the downward side or has been quiet, and other important characteristics.

Turning points, too, vary in time and volume. There cannot be, of course, any set type. Ordinarily, turning points are distributive or accumulative. I am writing now of turning points within major trends, although major-cycle turning points, also, are unquestionably distributive at the tops. Consequently, the time the activity consumes, and the amount of activity which occurs at distribution points, depend upon the amount of stock to be distributed, which can be judged only by familiarity with, and close study of, the preceding action.

Obviously, volume which may be important in stocks with small capitalization will be negligible where large outstanding issues of common stock exist: for example, the significance and the effect of a 5,000 share trade in Auburn Auto, with 185,000 shares outstanding, would be far different from those of a like transaction in General Motors, with 43,000,000 shares.

Another factor enters here: the number of people trading. Thousands of traders desert the market after a severe break; others become disgusted and trade only occasionally. There is another large group who become involuntary investors. Thereafter the number of active traders gradually increases, which fact may be sensed from our contacts in offices, from our reading, from statistics, and from the increases in average daily volume.

During the final stages of a bear market we hear a great deal about pools' being unable to attract a public following. The important pools and syndicates, whose objectives are large profits, are not desirous of attracting an active public following during the period when they are accumulating stocks, but prefer that the public gradually increase in participation and enter the market actively when prices are materially higher.

Important, or "Good" Buying and Selling

You often read that "good buying was apparent on the tape today." It is my opinion that this phrase is used too loosely at times by financial writers, because it is probably the most difficult conclusion to arrive at correctly from reading the tape. A definition of "good buying" is necessary. I understand it to mean buying by important interests—perhaps institutional invest-ment-buying, or purchases made by some banking group.

Also, pool accumulation would be called good, or important, buying, in that the pool would buy with the purpose of holding for a substantial advance. Opposed to this good buying, are the purchases made by the short interests in the market, who buy to cover their previous short sales. Likewise, speculative buying by scalpers, who take profits of one and two points, could not be called good buying.

Broadly stated, good buying absorbs stocks which will not be thrown upon the market at the first signs of a rally. Sometimes, of course, a banking group who are sponsors for a stock will support their stock with purchase orders, and will expect to sell all or a part of the stock when the market rallies; but, having supported the stock, they would not sell the next day, as it would undo the good they had done.

Important selling, on the other hand, comprises liquidation of important accounts, as contrasted with marginal selling, which originates from overextended trading accounts and from fear on the part of the public.

Indications on the tape which would tell the tape reader whether the buying or selling is important or not, are difficult to make out. The important time to look for them is following either a substantial reaction or a substantial rally. What the vol-ume alone tells us is not always a dependable index; so we have to look at price action as well. Short-covering plus speculative buying, following a decline or reaction, causes faster price-ac-tion than investment buying. The rally may be started by support buying, investment buying, short-covering, or a combination of all three. The action at the turning-point has been well covered in previous illustrations. After the turn, the extent and character of the movement tells the tale. An exceedingly rapid recovery denotes short-covering, or buying for a quick turn, or often both. A more gradual advance with constant volume of transactions, as opposed to spurts and wide price-changes, indicates a better quality of buying.

After the initial rally, watch the secondary reaction, if one occurs, for the character of the price changes and of the volume. During the stabilization periods preparatory to a further advance, you may be able to detect important blocks taken here and there. By and large, the distinction is fine, except in those apparent cases where the market rallies in points between sales; then, of course, you know it is mostly short-covering, and that it cannot hold. Do not overstay these sudden rallies (or fast reactions, if you are short); they have a habit of dying out suddenly.

Margin selling, as contrasted with liquidation, has similar ear-marks. The pace is swifter, and prices drop rapidly between sales. Liquidation is more persistent than margin selling, and is broader. Margin selling usually affects more swiftly those leading stocks which are widely held on margin.

Wild price movements during a rally indicate a meager supply of stocks. Those who have stock for sale quite naturally revise their selling prices when they see a rally start; offers are withdrawn, and buyers are forced to bid sharply for stock. Investment buyers and other groups who wish to buy stocks for accumulation, are slow to bid up prices, often buying "on a scale down." Consequently, their orders may be noticed on reactions, when they are filled quietly at more favorable prices.

It is well to remember, too, that we must be quicker to catch rallies and reactions when the public is heavily in the market.

WITHDRAWING BIDS

Just as offerings are withdrawn, so are bids often pulled from the market. You would not allow your bid at 88½ to remain in for a certain stock if the action of the market indicated to you that your choice might be available at 86.

This brings up another point which bears careful watching. Large bids, or offerings, are often placed with the specialists, which facts are noised about and transmitted to brokers' offices for the sole purpose of fooling the public. In October, 1930, it was widely circulated that there were orders for 50,000 shares of Steel at 150, when X was selling at 151 or 152. When Steel broke through 150 it was on sales of only a few hundred shares. Whether the bids were ever placed for the huge blocks, I do not know; but if they were, they were withdrawn.

A similar occurrence happened with Standard Oil of New Jersey, in October, 1930. In 1929, you remember, the Rockefellers were reputed to have offered $50 per share for 1,000,000 shares of "Jersey." A year later, when the stock again had declined to 51 or so, it was reported that there were orders totalling 150,000 shares at 50. The stock went through 50 without anywhere near 150,000 shares being purchased. It also, about a month later, again plunged through 50 without any great difficulty.

Occasionally bids of this character are beneficial, but many times they are harmful. Remember also that support in times of distress is only temporary, and that stock purchased for support purposes comes back on the market.

Another stunt is for brokers to call out: "Whitney is buying Steel," or: "Meehan is buying Radio," or: "Danforth is selling XYZ." Let us bear in mind that barring the possibility that Mr. Whitney might wish to have it known that he is buying Steel for the purpose of support during a crash, none of these big floor traders or operators will allow his movements to be heralded, unless his so doing aids his maneuvers. And why should he? Let us not forget that when Mr. Big Operator is selling a stock *publicly*, and is thoughtful enough to tell us about it, he may be *buying more than he is selling*, through several other brokers.

I was told recently that Jesse Livermore has no regular brokerage accounts, but drops in at this broker's and that, leaving orders to buy or sell. He may sell 5,000 shares of some stock one day in a Palm Beach branch office and buy the next morning in Miami. But, the tape will record his orders. It is up to us to guess whether the balance is on the buying side or the selling.

Think in Dollars, Not in Points

I have mentioned earlier in this part of the book the value of thinking in terms of dollars rather than in points. I believe in it thoroughly, as I know that it brings home the incidents which may be reflected on the tape. The next time you are watching one of your stocks, notice the volume, and, as the record passes before you, quickly calculate the transactions into dollars of volume. I believe that you will get a better sense of the action of the volume if you do this.

Chapter 12
The Effect of News on Market Action

To sell on good news is a broad recommendation. The trouble with this lies in the difficulty of distinguishing between *plain* good news and the good news. During a pool operation there will be plenty of news printed in the papers and over the Dow Jones tickers in reference to the stock. I have covered this subject of stock merchandising in Part One of this book. What we are interested in here is: how may we know when the news we read is the signal we have been waiting for, and what will the tape indicate?

Our dependable guide, volume, will aid us again. Watch your volume. Note from the action of the market how your stock reacts to any news you may read. Again you must decide whether you are trading on the intermediate trends or the shorter terms. The intermediate trend, naturally, will culminate upon more important news than the minor movements. Perhaps the big news is a stock dividend or a generous extra disbursement to stockholders which the insiders knew would be declared. Lesser news will have been circulated prior to the big event: information given to the press about increased profits, large orders, and including optimistic statements by the president.

Note the action upon the tape. See if the activity increases appreciably. When a piece of news breaks which you are *sure* is the important event, check back quickly over past action; determine whether the stock has been run up actively on increased volume. You may rest assured that if the news is *the* news upon which the pool has been operating, your tape will tell the story. It cannot help it. If the pool wishes to distribute stock, it must attract a public following; and a following cannot be attracted without increased activity. Rising prices, high volume, judicious doses of propaganda, and the big event: there is your program. (I refer you to Part One for a complete illustration of the distributive steps.) We can detect the success or failure of the pool's plan (and many pools fail in their operations) *only by the volume of business they are able to do.* Do not forget for an instant that they must sell what they have purchased, if they are to make profits. It is up to you and to me to ascertain if they are successful merchants.

Moreover, the general market must be right. No pool can distribute stocks profitably in a technically weak market. They would not try it. Therefore analyze your market, your individual stock, and judge the effect of news from the tape. But, when you decide to sell, sell quickly; do not wait for *unnecessary* confirmation. If you do, you will lose many dollars of profits. If you are not sure, sell anyway and let the others try for the top.

News is discounted; that is why a stock will generally act contrary to what is expected. After a long decline in its stock, for example, a corporation may pass the dividend. Instead of declining much further, the stock stabilizes and later advances. Naturally, the important selling, on behalf of those who were in a position to know the actual condition of the company's earnings, has been proceeding for weeks, or maybe months. National events, increased business, world conditions—all of these are judged in advance by intelligent investors, bankers, and big operators. They know how the public will react; they realize that the time to buy is when the public sells—on bad news—and that the time to sell is when the public buys—on good news.

A sudden, unexpected event cannot be discounted. I touch upon the Reserve Board warnings in 1929 on page 155. Wars, assassinations of public leaders, unexpected election results, sudden catastrophes: these are a few of the occurrences which are not discounted in the market.

When any of these happens, stop and think what the majority will do; also estimate the seriousness, the *extent* of the effect of the incident. Then decide upon your course of action, being careful not to do the expected thing. If you cannot make up your mind, do nothing but watch the tape, which will tell you what the opinions of other buyers and sellers are. Dumping of stocks means that the public is selling; persistent pressure is a sign that intelligent selling is taking place. Sell with the intelligent; and enter your purchase-orders when you notice intelligent, important buying.

CHAPTER 13

RESISTANCES

RESISTANCE AND SUPPORT LEVELS

During all movements of stocks, whether up or down, there are repeated resistance levels. There are a number of different causes for them, and, likewise, their effects are quite different.

It is difficult to find the exact reason why a certain stock should meet resistance at 52 one day and at 56 a week later. However, if we picture the thousands of people—perhaps millions during roaring bull markets—who are interested actively in the market, and add the pool, professional, and banking elements, we have a large number of situations something like this:

The Buying Side Those:
who are buying today.
who are covering short sales.
whose buying "stop" orders will be executed.
who have orders in at lower prices.
who have orders placed at higher prices.
who sold lower down, and wish to buy.
who sold higher and wish to buy.

The Selling Side Those:
who are selling long stock.
who are selling short.
whose selling "stops" will be executed.
who have orders in to sell at higher prices.
who bought higher up and will sell.
who bought lower down and will sell.

Among these multitudes of orders there are countless variances in decisions about where to buy and where to sell. There are innumerable levels at which opinions momentarily are evenly balanced—where demand and supply will balance. Possibly the resistance will be for only a few minutes, when the sellers will become more numerous·than the buyers (in quantity of orders, not in number of persons). As the stock declines we will say, demand increases and a stronger resistance is set up. Conversely, as the stock advances, more and more sellers offer stock for sale. In our example of Loew's (Chapter 8) there was quite a sizable resistance at the 58 level for several days, and a much more tenacious resistance within the broader range of 57 to 63.

A hard and fast rule cannot be laid down as to where resistances will occur. You must depend upon the action of the market—the action of the volume—to indicate the resistance levels. Upon many occasions a resistance will be set up at a point 50 percent of the way between the limits of the previous move. In other words, if a stock has rallied from 40 to 60 and then reacted, it may stop at about 50. Although I have never been able to determine satisfactorily why this so often happens, I imagine it to be simply a matter of the law of averages working between the sellers and buyers. However, this 50-percent-resistance rule fails so often that it cannot be considered reliable. One method which may be adopted, is to watch the action of the volume at the 50-percent level. If volume dries up as it approaches this level, or, on the other hand, if the volume is heavy at that point but the stock fails to go through, you have a dependable resistance.

In the day's chart of Loew's (page 46) there was a good deal of stock offered for sale at 58 and thereabouts; several times during the day, buying-orders pushed the stock up to that point only to meet a greater supply. There was evidently resistance to selling pressure also, or, I should say, a lack of selling pressure, when the stock returned to the 56-57 level. This is getting down very fine, and is of interest only to the daily scalper. Nevertheless, the same principles hold true at more important resistances.

No mechanical resistances are absolutely dependable. Some stocks will advance ten points and react only three, while others will fall back half-way. Of course, behind the market action you have the actions of buyers and sellers, plus, in the case of a pool-operation, the efforts of the pool. No pool manager is going to operate a stock in exactly the same manner each time; nor is he going to allow the stock of its own accord to rally and react in uniform movements. If he did, it would be too easy for you and me to learn the stock's characteristics, shut our eyes, and reap the harvest.

However—and this is highly important—each operator has certain modes of action, which, unless he is particularly shrewd, will occur and recur. He is quite likely to employ the same maneuvers again and again. If we can become well enough acquainted with his methods, through studying the stock, we may be able to detect far more accurately the various resistance levels. When he is accumulating his stock, he will endeavor to make it appear unattractive; contrariwise, when he is selling, he will try to induce us to buy. Stock exchange rules concerning false manipulation are so strict that not many operators attempt unethical practices. In active stocks, all pool maneuvers will appear on the tape. Of course, a pool manager may be able to buy, or sell, a block of stock outside; but he must make the stock active if he is to gain a public following.

If you will keep charts showing the daily high and low ranges of the stocks in which you are interested, plus a number of the market leaders, and then study your tape action, you doubtless will be able to determine resistance points. However, they will vary from time to time; never depend upon them mechanically, remembering that human beings, not robots, are buying and selling stocks. Estimate all of the resistances you want to from your charts, but notice *where* the volume comes in testing your resistances. Volume indicators on daily charts will be an aid, but they will not show you where or how within the day's range the volume occurred.

Congestion levels, where stocks have remained for periods of time, usually resist the move when the stock again approaches them. During the bear market, there were numbers of these congestion levels which acted as temporary stopping places in the downward decline. These become resistances to the advance when the trend is reversed. However, another point must be borne in mind here: resistance levels lose their power of resistance in proportion to the *time* which separates them. A congestion level, for example, which is formed in July, is not particularly efficacious six months later.

Support levels are levels at which supporting orders come into the market, and are often where reactions have met support before, although the farther away in time they are, the less dependable. They are verified in the same manner as resistance levels. Volume is the indicator of their importance. Surely a support level is not dependable if a stock will penetrate it for five points under either heavy or light volume. Its stubborn defense is confirmed when it holds against an assault; and if it breaks after holding for a long time, the plunge may be deeper than if it had given way under the first drive.

You can easily see why. If you were supporting a stock, if you believed that you had sufficient capital to withstand the selling orders you judged would come into the market at that level, you would attempt it. If, however, the supply of stock for sale increased, you would undoubtedly step aside and decide to enter your support farther down. This is what happened in the Electric Power and Light situation (page 57). If, in the mean time, you had misjudged the supply and had already used a large portion of your capital in the unsuccessful support, you would not have the capital to support the stock again until the selling was fairly well exhausted.

How can we hope to guess these things? How can we learn what is going on except by watching the battle? In modern army tactics every maneuver and every skirmish is planned to accomplish an objective. Various maneuvers or skirmishes are employed to obtain information about a most important factor—the strength of the enemy troops. (In stock market speculation, for example, an operator may test strength by selling a large block of stock and, if this is readily absorbed, then switch his position and "go long.") Having ascertained the enemy's strength, the general must know if he has sufficient support troops (in speculation, sufficient buying-power) to gain his objective. An army is only as strong as its support troops. Having worn down the enemy's resistance, shock troops are then employed to carry out the objective.

Is not financial strategy exactly the same? The tape is your scout. It prints the number of soldiers marshalled for the combat. If the enemy continues to pour army after army into the breach, he will penetrate the lines. His disregard for the expenditure of life (dollars, in our case) may cause a great difference in his maneuvers later; but we are interested in the immediate, as well as the future, battle. A financial general advances and retreats, sends out scouts, tests the enemy's lines of resistance, builds fake trenches, and plans his maneuvers just as cleverly and skillfully as the general in war time.

Use charts; employ every aid you can think of. But remember that your charts are records only of *past* human action. Your charts are pictures of the *results* of financial strategy.

I wish to give one more army illustration: there is many a skirmish in the front lines which to the untutored would appear to have little to do with the bigger movement on foot. However, the general, from his vantage-point, planned that skirmish with a knowledge of the effect it would have on the bigger plans ahead. So it is with the difficult-to-notice fluctuations on the tape, which, when accompanied by certain volume signals, may indicate important moves pending.

I believe that the 2,300-share transaction in Loew's on Saturday morning, November 15, which is discussed on page 44, was a skirmish indicative of something better to come. It caught my attention at once; and, as I had felt would be the result, activity soon picked up at advancing prices. I feel sure that that particular transaction was of great importance. Whether it indicated a final "mopping-up" of the necessitous liquidation which evidently had gone on previously, I do not know; but I do know that, coming as it did when the stock had been quiet and dull, it certainly was a signal. The confirmation, that it was intelligent buying, followed.

Retreats in the night with surprises in the morning, are as common in the market as in battle. Likewise, a masterly marshalling of dollars at the close of an active day may be counted upon to bring the enemy into combat in the morning.

I dwell upon this subject of maneuvers at length because it is of an importance which cannot be over-emphasized.

Inasmuch as I personally do not trade in and out of the market for a dollar profit here and fifty cents there, I do not pay a great deal of attention to minor resistance points, except in so far as they may represent a skirmish which is part of a major battle.

As I have mentioned before, I owned some shares of Loew's at the time that I kept track of the day's transactions in that stock. I was interested in its action, even at minor points, because of the fact that a few days previous it had suddenly reversed its trend, and, although I felt it would soon resume its upward course, I wished to check its movements and action carefully during that critical period. If it had shown signs of continued weakness, I should not have hesitated to throw it out at once and accept the loss.

Old Highs and Lows

Sometimes old highs and lows are resistance points, and often they are not. An old low means nothing in itself. If the action of the market indicates resistance at that level, well and good. It is the action which must give you your answer. In the fall of 1930 many people thought that the low point established in November, 1929, would be a resistance point against a further decline of the general market. As far as I could see, there was no apparent change in the market when it went through those year-old lows. And why should there be? The conditions, fortunes, and mental reactions of the people certainly underwent tremendous changes during the year 1930, and there was no reason for assuming that the old levels would set up any actual resistance. The market also was greatly changed in that year. Many groups which make up the general averages of the whole market, had long before declined below their individual 1929 levels, whereas other groups were still well above. The entire situation was different in all respects, and could not be compared.

Previous lows and highs which are nearest by—that is, which have been recorded a short time before the action you are studying—may be of some importance. I say "may be" because they have failed so many times to mark resistance, that I do not feel they are important, except as points to watch on the tape and *then* judge.

My belief is that all so-called mechanical points are dangerous until they are confirmed by the action of the stock itself. If any of the theories we hear about ever did work consistently, they could not do so for long, because too many traders would soon be acting on them, and their effectiveness would thus be ruined. Resistance is a temporary balancing of power. If we all played for a given resistance, there would not be any resistance left when the stock arrived at the expected point, because all of us would have executed our orders ahead of it, in order to take advantage of it.

CHAPTER 14
SUGGESTIONS TO SPECULATORS

BE A CYNIC WHEN READING THE TAPE

We must be cynics when reading the tape. I do not mean that we should be pessimists, because we must have open minds always, without preconceived opinions. An inveterate bull, or bear, cannot hope to *trade* successfully. The long-pull investor may never be anything but a bull, and, if he hangs on *long* enough, will probably come out all right. But a trader should be a cynic. Doubt all before you believe anything. Realize that you are playing the coldest, bitterest game in the world.

Almost anything is fair in stock trading. The whole idea is to outsmart the other fellow. It is a game of checkers with the big fellows playing against the public. Many a false move is engineered to catch our kings. The operators have the advantage in that the public is generally wrong.

They are at a disadvantage in that they must put up the capital; they risk fortunes on their judgment of conditions. We, on the other hand, who buy and sell in small lots, must learn to tag along with the insiders while they are accumulating and running up their stocks; but we must get out quickly when they do. We cannot hope to be successful unless we are willing to study and practice—and take losses!

But you will find so much in Part Three of this book about taking losses, about limiting losses and allowing profits to run, that I shall not take up your thought with the matter now.

So, say I, let us be hard-boiled cynics, believing nothing but what the action of the market tells us. If we can determine the supply and demand which exists for stocks, we need not know anything else.

If you had 10,000 shares of some stock to sell, you would adopt tactics, maneuver false moves, throw out information, and act in a manner to indicate that you wanted to buy, rather than sell; would you not? Put yourself in the position of the other fellow. Think what you would do if you were in his position. If you are contemplating a purchase, stop to think whether, if you act *contrary* to your inclination, you would not be doing the wiser thing, remembering that the public is usually wrong.

Use Pad and Pencil

If you wish to "see" market action develop before your eyes, I suggest that you adopt the use of pad and pencil. Many of us find it difficult to concentrate; but I know that I have often missed important action in a stock because I did not concentrate. Try the pad-and-pencil idea; keep track of every transaction in some stock. Write down in a column the various trades and the volume, thus: 3—57½ (meaning 300 shares at $57.50). When strings appear, write them as connected sales so that you may analyze them later. Note particularly the larger blocks. Reflect upon the result of these volume-sales; note where they came.

It is remarkable what this practice will do for one's perception. I find that it not only increases greatly my power of observation, but, more important still, that it also gives me, somehow, a commanding grasp of the action which I should not otherwise have. Furthermore, I am certain that few persons can, without having had much practice at it, remember accurately where within the action the volume came.

If you cannot spare the time to sit over the tape for this practice, you can arrange with your broker to obtain the daily reports of stock sales of the New York Stock Exchange. They are published for every market day by Francis Emory Fitch, Incorporated, New York City. Each transaction is given, with the number of shares traded and the price. From these sheets you can make charts of every transaction, and study where the volume increased or dried up, and the action which followed.

I know of no better training than to practice forecasting future movements from these charts and then check up to see if you have judged correctly. When you miss, go back over your previous days' action, and see if the signals were not there but that you misinterpreted them. It is so easy to undervalue some very important action that some such method is necessary. I have found this one to give splendid training, and I use it constantly.

Trade Alone

This counsel may be the most important I can suggest: trade alone. Close your mind to the opinions of others; pay no attention to outside influences. Disregard reports, rumors, and idle boardroom chatter. If you are going to trade actively, and are going to employ your own judgment, then, for heaven's sake, stand or fall by your own opinions. If you wish to follow someone else, that is all right; in that case, follow him and do not interject your own ideas. He must be free to act as he thinks best; just so must you when trading on your own initiative.

You may see something in the action of a stock that some other chap does not notice. How, then, can he possibly help you if you are making a decision upon some occurrence which you have studied but which he has never observed? You will find hundreds of people ready to give you free advice; they will give it to you without your asking, if you raise your eyebrow or look in their direction. Be a clam, an unpleasant cynic.

Have no public opinions of your own, when asked; and ask for none. If you get into the habit of giving opinions you are inviting an argument at once. You may talk yourself out of a decision which was correct; you will become wishy-washy in your conclusions, because you will be afraid of giving an opinion which may turn out wrong. Soon you will be straddling the fence in your own mind; and you cannot make money in trading unless you can come to a decision. Likewise, you cannot analyze tape action and at the same time listen to 42 people discussing the effects of brokers' loans, the wheat market, the price of silver in India, and the fact that Mr. Raskob and Mr. Durant are bullish.

Dull markets are puzzling to traders, doubtless because it is difficult to rivet the attention on the tape when it is inactive. If the tape bores you, leave it alone; go out and play parchesi—do anything but join in the idle, unintelligent gossip in a broker's boardroom.

Use a pad and pencil, as I suggested. It will occupy your mind and concentrate your attention. Try it; you will not be able to chatter and keep track of trades at the same time.

I may seem to write acidly here, but I have been through it, and have been one of the worst offenders. It was great fun to strut my opinions, but it increased the amount of red ink in my account; I know that. The worst of it is that I unconsciously may have hurt someone else when I participated in boardroom talk, to say nothing of unsettling my own thinking.

Do Not Watch Every Stock

Just as I urged you several pages back to watch Steel, so do I beseech you now not to try to watch too many stocks. It cannot be done. If you are going to keep accurate account, mentally, of volume and of the condition of supply and demand, you must perforce concentrate. Do not attempt to watch more than three stocks in addition to Steel; certainly not more than five. Many successful traders operate in only one stock; but they know that one.

To be successful, we must become thoroughly acquainted with our trading stocks; we must learn their peculiarities, must determine their resistances and so-called support levels. We must watch for important transactions, to note *where* within the day's range the volume comes.

Unless we have unusual minds, it is impossible for us to retain, and register, the action of more than from three to five stocks.

THE USE OF CHARTS AND STATISTICS IN
CONJUNCTION WITH THE TAPE

The interest in charts is so widespread that I believe some reference should be made to them. There are various kinds: daily, weekly, and monthly. Some traders chart even hourly action.

A chart of daily action is probably the most satisfactory, although for tape-study I have recommended that charts be kept of every transaction for practice in observation and perception. It would be difficult to keep any quantity of these latter graphs, because of the time it takes to make them.

A chart of daily action presents a clear picture of the position and previous action of active stocks. The chief value of charts lies in their enabling one the more easily to judge the *trend*. There are also many other indications which the charts give us, and which, when checked with the tape, are of value to the trader. However, many traders employ them mechanically and do not seem to realize that a chart is nothing more than the day's combined opinions of buyers and sellers of stocks. If the underlying human motives are understood, and if it is recognized that there is no sure-fire system which may be "played," charts are invaluable.

In *Stock Market Theory and Practice*, a recent book on the market, Schabacker discusses chart formations and their interpretative value. I refer you to this book; the author's explanations of charts and their uses, are detailed and clear-cut, and are supported by countless illustrations of the various movements.

I have heard traders claim that they do not need charts because they fix in their minds a picture of the previous action of the stocks in which they are interested. I seriously doubt if it is humanly possible to retain accurately in one's mind the previous action, and the present position as it is compared to the previous action, of one stock, to say nothing of that of fifty or a hundred stocks.

The use of statistics and a knowledge of investment fundamentals are, of course, accepted as necessary to participation in the market. So many adequate books have been written on the economics of investment that it would be presumptuous of me to attempt to cover the ground again here. Naturally, I urge the use of both by the trader on the intermediate trends. However, I doubt if the daily speculator can use statistics. Surely the statistical position of a company, or of general business, can have little to do with the minor fluctuations of stock prices.

The intermediate trends, however, are often affected by the quarterly earnings of corporations (which, remember, are discounted in advance of their publication) and by the condition of business generally. The money-market, the credit situation, the commodity markets, and other related commercial and industrial factors, all must be given their weight in judging and forecasting the trends of stock prices.

Here again, however, we may turn to the tape for the result. The market reflects all of these fundamentals, and discounts improvements or set-backs in general conditions. Individual corporate situations, likewise, are reflected in advance in the action of the market.

Statistics are past history; this fact must never be lost sight of. The earnings of the last quarter, when published, have little to do with the market action at the time of reading. They are of value in estimating present and future earnings, which the market is discounting. Never buy and sell on the basis of past history, except when you are selling to discount the good news which is finally released, or are buying when the uncertainty, or poor report, is removed.

In bear markets prices do decline on bad news, and rally on good news. Inasmuch as 1930 is behind us, I see little to be gained from a detailed discussion here of how to combat a bear market, other than the knowledge that we must watch the volume and trade with the trend, which I have already elaborated upon. It is an accepted theory that it is safe to make investments in a bear market when the market ceases to decline on bad news.

The tape student will find it difficult at first to correlate all of the various factors which are reflected on the tape; but as his knowledge and study widens, he will learn the key point: discounting. Volume activity will show him the extent of the enthusiasm or pessimism of all buyers and sellers.

ACTING CONTRARY TO THE PUBLIC

The question when to act contrary to the public, is a difficult one to answer. At important *turning points*, I believe it is safe to state, the public is *always* wrong—that is, the majority. As I stated on page 28, I adopted this theory in November, 1930, to detect the temporary bottom of the long decline. The public wanted to go short at the bottom. Prices had sagged for so long a period that it was finally considered that short sales were the only way to make money. However, when *everyone* wants to buy, or when everyone wants to sell, look out!

During the intervening movements, however, it is more difficult to determine the best course to pursue, whether to follow your inclinations or act contrary to them. For example, when, after prices have been rallying for some time, a reaction sets in and margin accounts *start* selling, it would not be wise to buy. First, we must determine the extent of the reaction; we must time our purchases so as to buy when the selling wave appears exhausted. Contrariwise, we should sell *before* the public on the signal of the increased volume and price activity which mark turning points, and not wait to go in the opposite direction at the first signs that the public is selling.

I wonder if I have made this clear. Perhaps a few more examples will help to straighten this thought out. I feel that it is very important, inasmuch as I know that I have blindly gone contrary to my first inclinations at times, only to learn afterward that I should have followed my first thought and gone *with* the public for a part of the way, and then "crossed" them later at the strategic hour.

Do you remember the several sudden breaks during 1929? There were a number which were caused by the warnings of the Federal Reserve Boards. The Boards withheld their announcements until after the close of the markets. In those cases the wise course to pursue would have been to stop and ask ourselves: "What will the rank and file do in the morning? Will they sell at the opening?" Then, it would have been necessary to act in a fashion contrary to that of the public.

In several instances which I recall, stocks opened considerably off in the morning, but, so soon as the selling had been absorbed, started their advance once more. The profitable move then would have been to buy upon the confirmative signs of the heavy volume of selling-orders being well taken—when the important buying appeared and demand overcame supply. The signs were there. We had the active churning of stocks without further progress on the downward side.

Over the long pull—even over the major intermediate movements—you can safely cross the public and make money. The ideal situation is a result of your having timed your actions so that you precede the public in buying—that is, buy when stocks are being accumulated—then you can go along with the majority during the major portion of the advance, and can part company at definite signs of increased public participation without corresponding progress in the movement of the stock. The greatest public participation is near and at the tops, because, as we have learned, rising prices attract a following.

Trend Trading

Roughly speaking, there are three types of trends: the long-pull; the intermediate; and the immediate, or short-term. Conservative traders operate within the intermediate trends. These last for anywhere from two weeks to six months. They can be gauged with profitable accuracy, whereas the minor movements are hazardous, owing "to the fact that you must act so quickly in order to get in and out. A reaction of four points within an intermediate movement of fifty points, certainly is not worth playing for; yet it may appear attractive on the tape."

The danger lies in the fact that our conclusions are not usually formed instantaneously; by the time we have been attracted to the reaction and have decided to sell, the reaction is over. The intermediate trends, however, allow time for thoughtful consideration. The profitable portion of these moves is in the middle. In an irregular market, buy when the action confirms the trend, and sell *early*. In a one-way bull market, sell when there have been one or two days of rapid progress on heavy volume following an important, gradual advance. Let the other fellow have the top and bottom.

If you intend to trade with the intermediate moves, be careful that your constant tape watching does not throw you off. A *minor* movement on the tape may upset your calculations. There is no doubt in my mind that if you are going to attempt to play for the minor fluctuations you must sit over the tape all of the time; but I believe that you are better off to study the tape only occasionally, to check your position, if you are operating for the intermediate trends. The bigger the movement you are maneuvering for, the less important become the hourly fluctuations.

However, an occasional check-up is, of course, wise, to let yourself know of important changes and of any increase in volume activity; it will either confirm your judgment to stay with your commitment, or cause you to question your position. In the event that you notice something which does not look quite as you would like for it to, then, naturally, you will want to study the action more closely. If you do notice action which you do not entirely like, do not *hope*. Watch, analyze, study! Sell quickly if you think something unexpected has occurred. You can buy in again any time, but you cannot bring back profits which have been wiped out by a sudden, unforeseen reaction. You can wait, of course, for later profits; you can take a small loss and start over again; but there is nothing so satisfying as taking a well thought-out profit.

Remember, you are trading; it should never for a moment unsettle you to see a stock advance ten points just after you have sold it. Try again; check your judgment; perhaps you failed to notice the right signal. Never mind; the market will be open to-morrow. Remember that it is the time at which you enter your order, not the price you pay, which returns the profit.

Trade with the trend, not against it. This is so fundamental that it scarcely needs discussion, but I have seen many traders "buck" trends in their commitments. When you have determined in which direction lies the trend of your stock (and of the general market, for it seldom pays to trade in a stock which moves contrary to the market), place your orders. But, so soon as you think the trend has turned, sell quickly. Hundreds of losses have been incurred because it was *hoped* that the trend had not reversed.

Capitalization and Floating Supply

Stocks with large capitalization have greater floating supplies of stock in the hands of brokers and traders than do those whose capitalization is small. The ideal trading stock is one of which there is a large floating supply, which is being traded in constantly, and which is shown on the tape frequently. The larger the floating quantity of stock, the less will the stock gyrate abnormally. Naturally, it takes a great deal more buying to move a stock with a floating supply of 3,000,000 shares than it does one with only 100,000. Wild-swinging and mystery stocks are usually those of small capitalization. Stocks which will advance or drop perpendicularly ten to twenty points in one day, are dangerous trading mediums. However, they are very profitable for you if you are on the right side; they are very attractive to buy and hold when you believe the trend is up.

My theory is to buy them outright and hold on tight for the important move. They swing so widely that it is most difficult to catch the in-between moves. Furthermore, they will often destroy your appetite and cause you to lose valuable sleep, if you misjudge the time to buy.

Let me counsel you, therefore, to seek unusual situations among these wild stocks for outright purchases and limit your more active trading to the stocks which are more stable, which do not jump several points between sales. Steel, for example, seldom moves more than an eighth between trades; yet it enjoys exceedingly profitable moves. There are many stocks, of course, which are good trading mediums. Select two or three which are active, stable between sales, and popular with the public.

Naturally, you will first satisfy yourself as to the fundamental soundness of the stocks. If their future prospects are bright, they will undoubtedly have the sponsorship of strong banking interests and the steering of strong pools—a winning combination for the trader who can read the tape action.

Patience is a Market Virtue

As a final suggestion, may I record here my plea for market patience? If we all would trade *only* when the trend is definitely indicated and then patiently wait until the action signifies the probable termination of the move, how much larger our profits would be! Six to twelve successful trades in a year, based upon the important, intermediate trends will return far greater profits than countless attempts within the minor fluctuations, whereby a large number of losses must ensue and where the profits will be small.

Chapter 15

The Rise and Fall of Steel During a Normal Bull Movement

The following discussion of a four-month movement in Steel, exemplifies the application of the several tape reading principles outlined in this book, and will serve as a summing-up before my jury of readers.

For the purposes of this illustration, we may contend that the market during the period between December 23, 1929, and April 15, 1930, showed an average bull movement. True, it was not as sensational as some of the advances during 1928 or 1929; but the latter part of that great bull market was abnormal in its intensity, and it is quite unlikely that we shall witness the like again for some years.

I have had reproduced, in Plates 15 and 16, the daily ranges of United States Steel between December 26 and May 6. Unfortunately, it is impossible to show in chartform the individual transactions *within* the various days' ranges, because of the space this would require. Nevertheless, the principles of the significance of volume are clearly demonstrated in the illustrations. The purpose of showing this entire movement is to demonstrate in one example the different types of volume = activity.

I have marked off sections of the charts from "A" to "H" to facilitate the explanation, and to make it easier for the eye to travel from the volume-indicators at the bottom, to the high-low-and-closing graph above.

Section "A" comprises the congestion, or accumulation, area in Steel, following the rather swift decline from 189 on December 10. It will be noted that twice—on January 2 and 10—an advance was attempted on good volume, only to meet resistance just above 173. After see-sawing back and forth for several days, with the volume light, Steel pushed through the resistance and closed, on January 23, at 175. We had the volume signal of this move when the number of shares changing hands registered the largest total in more than a month.

The advance was steady ("B") until February 1, when the volume conspicuously dried up for three days, indicating either a resumption of the advance following the rest, or a downward movement if volume increased on the decline.

February 14 ("C") witnessed another advance, which, however, did not get very far, the volume on this day not being sufficient to penetrate above 189¼. Again Steel died at the top; but this time the subsequent reaction was soon marked by a big volume day (the 20th), and within three more days X touched a low of 176¾, $12.75 per share under the top of but a week before.

The congestion for the next month was uneventful ("D" on Plate 15 and "E" on Plate 16), the extent of activity denoting either one of two possibilities: accumulation for a further advance, or quiet liquidation. Until March 17 we could not have been sure of the outcome. It was possible that Steel would roll over (as it did in September, 1930; Plate 2), and that a broad top would be formed. Naturally, from the trading standpoint, it would have been wise to sell out and stand aside, awaiting a definite indication of what the next move would be.

The advance on the 17th, with a volume of more than 120,000 shares, and being firm and steady, was a definite signal that important buying had been taking place—not liquidation. Incidentally, the action at that point illustrates the principle of the sudden reversal of a sagging, or tired, movement.

The action following March 17 ("F") is interesting. If you will follow it day by day you will notice the volume picking up on the days when Steel forged ahead, and dropping sharply during the days of slight set-backs.

The April top was not particularly difficult to gauge ("G"). We had three different signals, one on April 2, when X abruptly reversed its action after it had headed into a new high the day before. From the tape, we should have had this indication, as a matter of fact, on the 1st, because there was heavy volume at the top of the day, and no further progress was made. Following this the stock became tired, and under the pressure of average volume was unable to struggle higher.

On April 16 it looked for a time as if Steel would duplicate its performance of March 17 and follow the preceding eight days' sagging trend with an advance into new territory. However, it was soon apparent that this time the action had been distributive; and under extremely heavy pressure from constant offerings of stock, it turned down to close the day at the bottom of the day's range. The following day, both buyers and sellers marked time, although on the tape the reactions were on heavier volume than the rallies. On the 21st, Monday, there was no question of the action. Although the day's volume did not reach 100,000 shares, sellers were offering stock all day.

The decline gathered momentum, as you will see, with the volume heavy during the latter part ("H"). Each day until May 5 the volume signals indicated still lower prices. On the 5th, however, we received the "sold-out" indication. Volume was tremendous, over 190,000 shares; yet, after plunging into a new low, and following a terrific churning of transactions, buying overcame selling, and active bidding for Steel soon sent it forward, to close the day at a price $1.50 per share higher than that of the afternoon before. This ended the spring cycle.

The student of the tape-reading principles outlined in this book will be interested in a much closer scrutiny of Steel's action than this I have written. However, my short review brings out the point that volume will give you indications of pending moves, often when nothing else will.

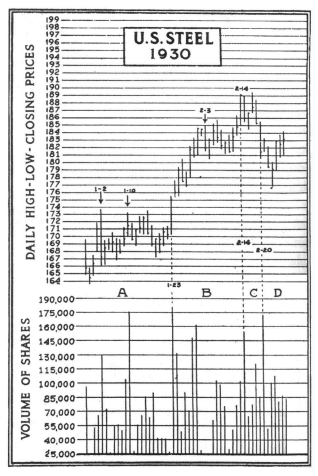

PLATE 15

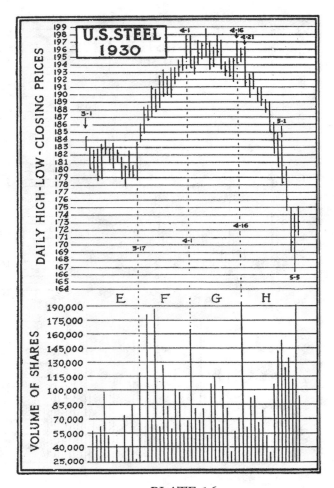

PLATE 16

PART THREE
MARKET PHILOSOPHY

CHAPTER 16

FOREWARD TO PART THREE

THE BIGGEST HANDICAP OF ALL IS OURSELVES

When we have mastered the intricacies of interpreting the market, we still have a long road to travel before we can expect success. The most difficult problem lies in ourselves. We may have reached sound conclusions concerning certain movements in stocks; our interpretations may be absolutely correct. Yet, we may lose money. Why? Because most of us cannot act in accordance with our own opinions! Where our own money is concerned, we allow personal hopes, fears, impatience, and vanity to cripple judgment.

The one thing which retards success in trading, more than any other, is the unwillingness of many of us to accept losses, cheerfully and quickly, when we realize that we have misjudged the action of the market. We will say to ourselves: That stock is not acting right; I believe it is going to decline.

Oh, well, I'll hold on a little longer; I guess it will advance later. We know far down inside ourselves that it is going to go against us, but our personal feelings prevent us from taking action.

MARKET PHILOSOPHY

In the years past I have written numbers of financial essays, or editorials, relating to characteristic trading frailties. In the pages following are collected a number of these "passing thoughts on human nature in finance," together with some reflections on other elements common to the stock market.

I can think of no better way of closing this introduction to a philosophy of stock trading than reprinting the ten rules which were written for me during the depth of the 1930 depression by one who styles himself "The Market Cynic:"

TEN WAYS TO LOSE MONEY ON WALL STREET
By The Market Cynic

After many hours of toil and deep thought I have compiled a dependable guide for stock traders: Ten Ways to Lose Money on Wall Street. I shall not attempt to explain or qualify these precepts, realizing that my readers will doubtless follow them regardless of any advice, from any source, to the contrary.

1. Put your trust in boardroom gossip.
2. Believe everything you hear, especially tips.
3. If you don't know—guess.
4. Follow the public.
5. Be impatient.
6. Greedily hang on for the top eighth.
7. Trade on thin margins.
8. Hold to your own opinion, right or wrong.
9. Never stay out of the market.
10. Accept small profits and large losses.

CHAPTER 17

THOUGHTS ON HUMAN NATURE AND SPECULATION

TRADE ON THE LONGER-TERM TRENDS

The average trader, because of the difficult task of successfully controlling his emotions, temperament, and characteristically human faults, has far greater chances for success if he trades on the longer-term movements of stock prices than if he attempts to trade in and out for small profits.

Trade for the larger intermediate-trend profits and limit your losses. That is the secret, if there is any. You will live more happily, worry less. You will gain market poise, will be able to act in accordance with your own dictates and will curb your natural impatience to jump in and out of trades thoughtlessly.

Finally: resolve, today, never, never to overtrade. Maintain, always, a margin of at least 50 percent.

MARKET POISE

As I wander about in and out of brokerage offices, I am struck with the looks on the faces of the traders sitting around the boardrooms. So many of them register fear, worry, and distrust when the market is going against them, and greed, lust, and superficial happiness when they have paper profits.

Speculation in stocks, to be successful, must include judgment, common sense, and market perception; whereas stock gambling is nothing more than guessing upon the tick of the quotations.

A speculator may some time acquire market poise, the stock gambler never.

When, after thoughtful deliberation and commonsense analysis, we come to the conclusion that a certain stock is undervalued—when we feel confident that its market action reflects intelligent accumulation—and we purchase it, we should be mentally at ease. Naturally, we shall be watchful for signs which may indicate that we have erred in judgment; but, with our having calmly considered all known factors, there is no reason for our lacking confidence or for being apprehensive of the outcome.

If, however, we stroll into a brokerage office and inquire of the first man we meet: "What's good for a turn this morning?" and then gamble on this information, we most certainly shall be upset and unhealthily nervous concerning the outcome.

In short, market poise is the result of a sense of mental well-being—confidence in the outcome of a speculative venture which has been entered into calmly, thoughtfully, and deliberately. If it should not work out profitably, as planned, and it is necessary to accept a small loss, this would not upset us, inasmuch as we should realize that we had applied our best judgment to the problem. We should appreciate that it is impossible to judge every market commitment correctly. Market poise is engendered by judgment, rather than by guess-work; by conservatism instead of rash chance-taking; by the willingness to remain on the sidelines when the issue between buyers and sellers is beclouded, rather than by feverishly demanding action at any cost.

There is No Such Thing as "Position"

To my mind there is no logic in a trader's talking about "losing his position" in a stock. An investor who is interested only in the long-pull trend, may be justified in considering his position, but not the trader.

I think you will agree with the statement that trading profits result from the accurate timing of commitments, and not from the prices paid. It makes not the slightest difference what prices you pay for your stocks when trading, if you so judge your purchases that you can later sell at a profit.

I have heard traders time and again justify their decisions to hold on to stocks which show them losses: because, they claim, they dare not take the chance of losing their positions. I reply to them emphatically that they are in *losing positions* right then. They have *already* lost money because of the positions they are in. Why, then, continue stubbornly to stick it out?

Recently I had the valuable opportunity to examine the complete records of a trader's account for the period between September, 1929, and September, 1930. On the whole he did not fare badly, but that was not the most interesting feature of his record. It was the conditions and results of his *losses* that interested me. Of the 148 instances in which his trades had gone "into the red," 110 of them were sold at losses larger than they would have been had he quickly limited each loss on the first indication that his trade was not working out as expected. Upon analysis I found that in nearly every case the substantial loss was caused by an opinion that, if he held his position, he would come out all right. In other words, when a commitment *started* in the red, only once in four times did it come out.

I realize that this was during a bear-market year, and that some readers will rise to inform me that, in a bull market, if we will hold on long enough we will not have any losses. A pretty theory, but it does not work. An examination of trading records will show that when small losses become large the average trader is quite likely to become frightened and sell. Ask your broker. He will tell you of the thousands of customers whom he has *sold out* because they hung on to their positions until the margin clerk politely, but firmly, removed them.

The only position I do not wish to lose is the position in a stock which shows me a profit. Then I shall try to hold on tight until my judgment tells me that I should do better to turn my paper figure into cash.

Reflected News

What kinds of news and reports are absorbed by the public and, consequently, are reflected in market movements?

Your average newspaper and magazine reader, first of all, does not retain what he reads. He skims through the papers, morning and evening; yet, were you to question him upon even the outstanding events of the day, he could give you at best only a garbled report of actual facts.

This holds true for the news on the financial pages, and for readers of financial magazines.

It seems to be a trait of human nature to remember what we want to remember and to gloss over facts which, although perhaps of greater importance, do not report favorably upon the subject we are interested in. What I am driving at is this: let us suppose that we own 50 shares of a chain-store stock, and our morning paper prints an article surveying the chain store situation. The analysis, if it is unbiased (which, sadly, is seldom so), will present both the favorable and the unfavorable facts.

It is a safe wager that unless we are on our guard—unless we practice concentration (this has become almost a lost art, has it not?)—we shall absorb only that portion of the article which lends weight to our previous judgment, employed when we purchased the stock; we shall not be interested, most probably, in the writer's unfavorable comments. Why? Because we own the stock, and do not wish to be told that we used poor judgment when we purchased it.

Psychologists tell us that a thought must be repeated again and again before the public as a whole retains it.

Likewise, the average investor had rather be *told* something, than dig it out of an article.

In consequence, there is little news which affects stock prices more than temporarily, until it has been repeated again and again. For example, brokers' loans are a weekly subject for conjecture; and traders speculate upon the effect brokers' loans will have on the market. (Do not miss that point—the effect the loans *will* have. In other words, the news after publication is of scant value, as intelligent opinion is registered *before* the facts are published.)

News flashed over the tickers has more effect, I believe, than magazine or newspaper articles. Occasionally a piece of news is sufficiently sensational to have an immediate effect on the market; the announcements of the Federal Reserve Board in 1929 are examples. Watch your step when these sudden announcements appear. However, they often have a more temporary, than lasting, effect. The Reserve warning in August, 1929, is illustrative of this. The lowest prices were registered in the first hour, and within a week or two stock prices had recorded new highs.

To my mind, news agencies owe a greater responsibility to their readers than is consistent with publishing sensational items which they must know are acted upon without deliberation by the thoughtless public. I criticize severely public men who, with their news agencies and propagandists, play upon public opinion without regard to the serious consequences which must ensue.

I should rest mighty uneasily at night if I knew that some remark or announcement of mine, which I had issued in order to parade my intelligence, had caused losses of millions of dollars to thousands of people who, *I knew, would act without thinking.*

The news of the market itself—the plus and minus signs—is unquestionably the most potent market factor. There is danger in this, and I shall try to point out how you may avoid certain pitfalls caused by the market's being its own best advertiser.

The Market as Its Own Best Advertiser

In the foregoing I touched upon the subject of market news— the plus and minus signs—being unquestionably the most potent factor in the market. I discussed the kinds of news and reports which are absorbed by the public and, consequently, are reflected in market movements.

An active, *rising* market, with a large volume of sales, attracts buyers. Public participation increases as prices advance. Peculiar as it may appear, the faster stock prices surge upward, the hungrier the public becomes for stocks.

In a declining market the same action holds true. As activity increases, more and more selling sets in: increasing numbers throw stocks into the whirlpool of liquidation. It is mob psychology: human nature reflecting its desire to follow. Schooled market operators and pool managers realize this fondness of the average investor to "get in on rising prices," and they use this powerful tool in their operations.

Perhaps you have seen the chart of a stock when, following a sharp advance, the curve of its daily action makes a saw-tooth formation. There will be a sharp dip lasting two or three days, followed by another spurt into higher ground. Another reaction sets in, again followed by a rally, which, however, may not reach the level of the previous advance. The formation may look like three cones, the middle cone higher than the one on either side.

What has happened? The insiders, or those who purchased thousands of shares of the stock at cheaper prices—perhaps pool operators—decide to sell, believing that the price of the stock has discounted reasonable future prospects. The advance of the stock, particularly the rapid action in the latter stages, has attracted a public following. Nevertheless, there are thousands of shares to be sold—distributed—and when heavy selling commences, the price breaks. It is necessary, then, for the operators to cease selling, and perhaps even buy more stock, in order that the public may not become worried. The price moves upward again, usually into new high levels, following which more stock is sold. The same procedure continues; but, strangely enough, the stock, after turning down from the third peak, often declines substantially, and there is generally a long period of comparative quiet before it again becomes active. The pool may again accumulate more stock and go through the same process. This is what is termed "accumulation and distribution." When the stock is distributed near and at the top it is said to be "passing from strong to weak hands, and its technical position thus becomes greatly weakened."

A conspicuous move in a market leader will often cause increased activity in a broad list of stocks. Financial writers often state that "under the leadership of such-and-such a stock the market advanced today."

You will see from the foregoing that it is wise to take bearings when you notice that stock prices have been advancing steadily for some days. Broadly speaking, fast action is indicative of the end of a move, as we have noted in the illustrations of top-action in Part Two.

THE TIME ELEMENT

"The Time Element" applies to the movements of stock prices.

Do you understand what is meant by the price structures of active stocks? Visualize ten thousand people, all of whom are either owners or prospective owners of a given stock. Of the owners, some have entered selling orders with brokers, setting a price at which each will sell. Others have entered stop-loss orders at varying fractions and points below the current market price.

Of those who are interested in buying the stock at a price, some have entered buying orders under the market, and some above the market (because, to the latter, if a stock breaks through a given range, it becomes a better purchase).

Thus we see that the market is honeycombed with buying and selling orders.

Now let us notice what happens following a rapid advance. The buying-orders *under* the market become of little value, *unless the stock reacts to its previous level*. If the stock rushes upward, there is not sufficient time to build up an underlying foundation of orders to check a decline, when it sets in. Conversely, of course, a sudden, swift decline obliterates the price structure also, as stop-loss orders are executed and the many buying-orders are withdrawn pending the "consolidation" of the stock's movements.

Stock prices move in accordance with supply and demand and in accordance with the *time* of previous movements. This is not mechanical in any sense, but psychological.

The more time a stock spends in a congestion period—in an area of closely lapped, daily price-ranges—the more pronounced will be the trend which follows. But, until the stock leaves its "pivot" you cannot be certain in which direction it will go.

Let me review with you hastily the movements of stock prices during the months of the 1929 break and the period following, and you will notice the value of the time element.

In the latter part of October, 1929, stock prices, as we well remember, declined with furious swiftness. Reason was thrown to the winds. Mob action, fear, and forced selling ruled the stock markets.

Buyers were scarce; consequently, stocks declined by many points between sales, instead of by the usual fractions of a point. On October 29 the first slide halted. Was that the time to rush in and buy? Not if you understood the importance of time as it relates to price-structures. You can see that it would be impossible to build a stabilizing market structure within only a few days after the panic.

Human beings need time for the return of reason following such shocks. How long did it take you to get over the emotional effect of the crash?

What happened? Another severe crash ensued; the swinging of stock prices proceeded, but each time the swings became narrower, until, at the end of December, 1929, and during January, 1930, stock prices stabilized and moved within a restricted area for several weeks. The advance from January forged consistently ahead, following the congestion, in proportion to the time of the stabilization. You will notice, however, that stock prices moved slowly; there were no signs of the past year's activity. Why was this? Because there was not sufficient time for the public to forget its losses and disappointments occasioned by the breaks, and to appraise the future; nor was there enough time to build up purchasing power.

How to Think, Market-Wise

In *Novum Organum*, Sir Francis Bacon estalished first his doubt of all things, before proceeding to his consideration of knowledge: "In general, let every student . . . take this as a rule that whatever his mind seizes and dwells upon with peculiar satisfaction, is to be held in suspicion; and that so much the more care is to be taken, in dealing with such questions, to keep the understanding even and clear. . . ."

The next time you receive a "hot" tip or read a piece of news in the paper, think it *through*. This is what I mean: in February of 1930, when a rather drastic cut in the cost of crude oil was announced, thousands of investors jumped to the conclusion that oil stocks would immediately go into a nose-dive. If they had thought through the problem, they would have asked themselves such questions as: Can the price cut be a bullish argument, in that the expected bad news is out? How much will the lower prices assist the campaign for curtailment of production? Will the price cut tend to hold production in line with consumption? Have leading oil stocks already declined as a result of over-production and its effects? Has the decline in oil stocks discounted possible lower earnings? Is it possible that the cut in crude oil prices is an argument for rising stock prices? Will gasoline consumption increase normally in 1930? If the cut in crude oil prices curtails production, what effect will this have on stock prices? Will curtailment in production now pave the way for increased crude oil prices later?

I could continue with two or three pages of questions, but you will get the idea from these few.

As Sir Francis Bacon wrote nearly three hundred years ago: "Doubt all before you believe anything! Watch your idols!" No better investment or trading counsel could be offered than this.

FUNDAMENTALS VERSUS TECHNICAL ACTION

There is a constant tug of minds between the school of counselors who claim that fundamentals are the only reliable barometers of future stock prices, and the so-called "technicians," who state that the action of a stock is an accurate index of its future movements.

Before we get into the discussion, let us quickly define "fundamentals." As commonly thought of, fundamentals are underlying factors. They include earnings reports, balance sheets, past history of the company's growth, management, accounting methods, position in its industry, public acceptance of its products, future earnings prospects, and other similar facts. In considering the general market, fundamentals would include credit and money conditions, domestic and foreign business activity, the import and export situations, the relation of leading stock prices to the prospective earnings of the corporations, and the like.

Can we, however, leave out the human equation? With the foregoing facts known, what basis is to be employed—what measuring stick is to be applied—to foretell accurately how these facts are going to affect the movements of stock prices? Shall we leave it to judgment, solely? If so, how are we to reconcile and justify the varying opinions of the *judges* of fundamental conditions?

How about the *action* of stocks? What does this tell us? A skilled analyst can detect technical factors, such as accumulation or distribution, the direction of the current trend, resistance levels, exhaustion and reversal of a trend, and other characteristic signals.

But wait a moment. What causes stock prices to advance and decline? The buying and selling of stocks, naturally. And, inasmuch as they are bought or sold by *people*, is not *human* action also a fundamental?

In short, is not the problem, in the final analysis, to determine what will be the public's and Wall Street's opinions of the commonly accepted fundamentals, as they are reflected in the market?

Therefore, why should there be any argument between the fundamentalists and the technicians? One supplements and complements the other.

There is still another angle to this question. The majority of the buying- and selling-orders in leading stocks do not come from investors, but are the result of speculation. This latter includes pool operations, professional trading, and the countless thousands of orders which are placed by those who are trying to scalp a point here and a half-point there. The effect of these orders must be considered when we are forecasting the future course of stock prices.

Therefore, it seems to me, all three factors—fundamentals, technical action, and market psychology—can, and should be, taken into account in the instance of each commitment. A complete analysis of the fundamental situation will tell us what should be expected, in our opinion. We shall thus find out what stocks appear attractive for investment.

Turning to a study of the past and of the current action of the stock under scrutiny (or the general market), we learn whether the *intelligent* agree with our opinion. We do not have to trust to personal judgment.

Technical signals likewise will advise us when to buy and when to sell. There certainly is a common meeting ground here. One cannot know too much about any investment situation. It was definitely proved in the fall of 1929 that conditions within the market itself—technical conditions—had as much to do with the extent of the crash as did fundamentals. However, from an unbiased study of both it was evident that stock prices were riding for a severe spill.

Market action is a *reflection* of fundamentals and of speculative and investment sentiment. How, then, can they be separated?

Pride of Opinion

Pride of opinion accounts for as many losses in the market as any other human factor that I can think of. When a man puts money into a stock upon his own judgment, or "guess," it is almost useless to attempt to show him that he has made a mistake and that he would be better off were he to switch into something else.

I suggest a solution for your consideration: the next time you buy any stock on your own judgment, or anyone else's, decide at that moment whether, if it turned down a certain number of points, instead of up, you would still have confidence in it. If you would not, then determine absolutely, right then and there, to sell it quickly. Do not wait until the stock has sagged before you figure out the wise move, but *decide before you buy it* exactly how you will feel if the unexpected happens; because, if you wait before making up your mind you will most likely dawdle and shilly-shally around. Before you know it you will be wishing you had acted differently, for you will be looking down at the stock and seeing unnecessarily large red figures, which will further upset you and doubtless will increase your loss.

Another point is: do not buy a stock and *then* ask someone what he thinks of it. If he disagrees with your judgment, you will not pay any attention to him anyway; and it is a waste of breath to run around looking solely for people who will agree with you. A friend once said to me: "I just bought some General Motors. What do you think of it? "I replied, quite nastily: "Why ask my opinion? You've already bought it. If I disagree with you, you'll think I don't know what I am talking about. Suppose, next time, you ask *before* you buy."

Pride of opinion obtains not only in the stock market. Ask a man who owns a Chevrolet what he thinks of it and he will tell you that it is the greatest car in the world. Later, when he graduates to a Buick, he will tell you that he does not know how he ever drove that tin-can Chevrolet, because, believe him, there is no car in the universe like the Buick!

For heaven's sake, remember that there are many good stocks. Your stock is not the only one which can go up and down. As a well-known operator has written, in *Watch Your Margin*, you do not need to have a love affair with your stock just because you bought it. Love is sometimes fickle, you know.

Many traders, because of losses from previous trades in a certain stock, feel that the stock "owes them something." They will take gambling risks in order to "get even:" I should say, in order to satisfy their pride or vanity, which, as Kelly states in *Why You Win or Lose*, is one of the four enemies to stock market success.

CHAPTER 18

MORE THOUGHTS ON HUMAN NATURE AND SPECULATION

GREED

I have watched traders in brokers' offices with deep interest, and have tried to learn the traits that crippled their profits. The desire to "make a killing"—greed—has impressed me particularly.

Perhaps this desire to squeeze the last point out of a trade is the most difficult to fight against. It is also the most dangerous. How often has it happened in your own case that you have entered a commitment with a conservatively set goal, which your judgment has told you was reasonable, only to throw over your resolutions when your stock has reached that point, because you thought "there were four more points in the move?" The irony of it is that seemingly nine times out of ten (I know, for it has happened with me) the stock does not reach your hoped-for objective; then—to add humiliation to lost profits—it goes against you for another number of points; and, like as not, you end up with no profit at all, or a loss.

Maybe it would help you if I told you what I have done to keep me in my traces: I have opened a simple set of books, just as if I were operating with money belonging to someone else. I have set down what would be considered a fair return on speculative capital, and have opened an account for losses as well as for gains, knowing that the real secret of speculative success lies in taking losses quickly when I think my judgment has been wrong. When a commitment is earning fair profits, and is acting as I had judged it should act, I let my profits run. But, so soon as I think that my opinion has been erroneous, I endeavor to get out quickly and not to allow my greed to force me to hold for those ephemeral, hoped-for points. Nor do I allow my pride to prevent an admission of error. I had rather, by far, accept the fact that I have been wrong than accept large losses.

Another helpful thing to do, especially when you feel in doubt about your position, is frequently to close out all commitments (except your investment backlogs) and stay out of the market for a time. This clears your perspective and allows your judgment to "congeal." Never hold to a position because of pride in an original conclusion which your later judgment whispers is wrong. If you will limit your losses quickly and allow your profits to run, you have to be right only two or three times in every five to earn extraordinary profits.

For fear of being misunderstood, I want to explain that the foregoing is not to be construed as advising daily scalping, or in-and-out trading "for a point," as, to my mind, there is nothing but grief to result from that in the long run. Rather, it offers suggestions for conservative speculation within the major or intermediate swings of stock prices. Concentrate your trading on these more important, intermediate moves and concentrate your mind on the *action of the stock*. Force yourself to forget "self" in order to trade in an impersonal, business-like manner.

Look Upon Your Stock Certificates as a Merchant Looks Upon His Merchandise

A merchant buys goods which he expects to *sell at a profit*. Your speculative purchases of stock certificates, to be successful, must be consistent with the same merchandising principle. Before you buy a stock, be satisfied that you can sell it to someone else at a higher price. Do not forget for a moment that for every share of stock sold there must be a buyer. I know that this sounds childish, but many evidently forget it. You do not make a *personal* sale when you sell your stock; simply, somebody somewhere buys it. It is your judgment, or your advisor's, which must decide whether there *is* somebody who will pay more for your merchandise than you did, plus your overhead expenses.

Likewise, just as a merchant knows that certain styles will not long remain in demand, so must speculators realize that certain stocks which are popular now, may lack demand three months hence. What does a merchant do when he learns that a certain coat which he has purchased does not sell readily? He immediately marks it down, let us say, 10 percent. Then, if after a few days it is still on his hands, he again lowers the price, until finally he may transfer it to the "basement bargains. "But *he sells that coat*—he does not hang on to it hoping that it will sell as originally priced.

If you are not familiar with retail merchandising, hunt up a friend of yours who is in the retail business—preferably women's wear—and ask him to tell you the principles of buying and selling for profit. I assure you that if you will do this and then thoughtfully consider the similarity of your market trading to retail trading, you will see the matter from a new and more profitable angle.

The most important factor in merchandising is the reading of the public's psychology of style, just as I claim that market, or investor, psychology is the most essential study in forecasting. There is an old saying in retail merchandising that "well bought is half sold." Is this not true of stocks? If your interpretation of market action—as it relates to demand—is correct, then your stock is half sold at a profit the moment you buy it.

Forget stock certificates as such and consider them as merchandise whose salability depends on fickle style. If you find that you have misjudged your market, offer your merchandise at cut prices and get rid of it. Take a loss and try again. Remember that if you limit your losses you can afford to accept many losses and still be ahead, because your correctly purchased merchandise will earn big profits for you.

Finally, do not try to sell winter coats in the spring. Sell them all before the last snow has gone. In other words, let your "competitors" have the last few points in a move. The surest profits are those in the middle—at neither the top nor the bottom.

Do Not Believe Anything You Read

Here are two headings which appeared over two practically identical financial articles, one published in *The Wall Street Journal*, the other in *The New York Times*, on Tuesday morning, July 29, 1930:

The Wall Street Journal:
Continental Oil 2nd Quarter Off; Consolidated Profit $2,120,518 Against $3,842,081 Year Ago; Six Months' Income Up

The New York Times:
Continental Oil's Net Profit Jumps; Quarter's Total Reported at $2,120,518 Against $523,302 in First Three Months. Big Curtailment Made; Company Forecasts Enviable Position When "Value for Products" is Received

It is not difficult to sense which newspaper was interested in publishing optimistic news. The remainders of the two articles were very much alike; doubtless each paper received the report from the company's publicity office. The headlines in *The Times* read as if they, also, were written in that office. These remarks are not made to render an opinion on Continental Oil stock one way or the other, but the illustrations are printed to point out that the unwary, thoughtless reader is at the mercy of the newspaper headline writer or a company's publicity man.

Actually, the only wise course to pursue in reading financial news is to believe nothing! Remember the wise counsel of Sir Francis Bacon: to "doubt all before you believe anything."

Bear in mind two important facts, facts which may cause your own downfall market-wise unless you are on your guard every minute.

First, newspapers, as a rule, do not wish to publish pessimistic news. Whenever possible the best foot is put forward in any piece of business reporting. Ask any publicity man and he will tell you that there is little use in sending any financial releases to newspapers, with the hope that they will be printed, unless they are optimistic in tone.

Second, corporations will seldom stress any but the best news of their operations. You constantly read news items about corporations, wherein new improvements, increased sales, new products, and what not, are reported. These items may be published purely for the purpose of interesting the public in the company's stock. Probably a pool is operating in the stock and it is soliciting the public's aid through advertising—the best advertising, next to rising stock prices on the ticker tape, being frequent news items.

A noted economist once told me that he tried never to believe anything he read in financial reports, but endeavored to place his own interpretation upon the facts and statistics published, paying no attention to the implied opinion of the writer. He admitted, however, that oftentimes he himself was carried away unwittingly by colorful reports which he did not analyze coldly and critically.

Referring again to the headlines at the beginning of this article, I wish to remark, lest you have not noticed it, that *The Times'* headline would imply a sensational increase in business if you saw only the report for the two quarters of 1930, although the half-year income was only slightly in excess of 1929 and the second quarter of 1930 was nearly two millions under the same period of the previous year.

A friend once sent me a clipping from the financial page of *The New York Herald Tribune*, which I reprint herewith. It hardly needs comment, for it simply bears out what I have said in this section:

The following two quotations, appearing in different newspapers yesterday, may, when taken together, help one understand just what went on in the stock market: "Operations for the rise," states one commentator, "which had been checked yesterday by profit-taking, were resumed with vigor on the Stock Exchange this morning and, despite further selling to realize profits, made excellent headway during the abbreviated session in a well diversified market." Exhibit No. 2: "Heavy selling went ahead in the principal industrial stocks in the weekend session. Uncertainty over the business outlook was induced by the recent bad breaks in cotton and wheat, and the decline in iron and steel prices."

I am told that many big operators scarcely ever read the financial pages of newspapers, because they wish to draw their own conclusions and formulate their own judgments from cold statistics and the action of the market, realizing that unconsciously they may be swayed by publicity releases and financial writers' opinions, which may be based upon hearsay rather than facts.

THE VALUE OF THE IMPERSONAL VIEWPOINT

If we all had the impersonal viewpoint concerning our investments and speculative commitments, I know that profits would be much larger, chiefly because losses would shrink. I honestly believe that the most important problem before both the investor and the speculator, is *limitation of losses*. In other words, the emphasis in the handling of all commitments should be put on the prevention of large losses and the willingness to accept *many small losses*.

We can do this only if we have the impersonal viewpoint. In your business, you doubtless never give a second thought to some small loss which your business judgment tells you to take, whereas if it were out of your own pocket you would have it on your mind all day. A merchant marks down a coat to move it quickly, but does not worry over the loss; a buyer, in a rush to get in some supplies, may find he has paid a few dollars more than would have been necessary if he had had the time to obtain several bids; a business man will spend the company's money for a trip which is not actually essential, but the expense will not worry him, although it indirectly may be his own money. In all these examples—and you can think of many more—the minds were focused upon the job in hand rather than upon the money expended.

How may you obtain this same viewpoint in the market? My only suggestion, which I have found works fairly well (not perfectly, I admit), is for you to look upon your market transactions, whether they are long-pull investments or commitments for the shorter swings, as simply constituting a business in which you are interested. Open a simple set of books, setting up a stipulated percentage of your capital (start with 33 1/3 percent) as a reserve against losses. Decide upon a conservative income from your investment, which will *not tempt you at any time* to become overextended. Open an account for surplus, and add to it each month (if you are actively trading) a specific percentage of your profits (at least 50 percent, which, in turn, should be invested in bonds or long-term common-stock investments).

I believe that, if you will do this, you will unconsciously find your mind to be upon the operation of your business, rather than upon the fact that each point means fifty or a hundred dollars in your pocket.

To return to the matter of limitation of losses: you will find that you are willing, even entirely satisfied, to accept a number of small losses, inasmuch as your mind will be focused *impersonally* on the business problem of adding to your surplus each month and as you will realize that you have a reserve against your losses which it is perfectly good business to use up, and because, if your percentages are worked out soundly, your losses are an expected and normal sequence in your business operation. In other words, to earn consistent profits you have to take losses, and many of them.

THE PUBLIC IS ALWAYS FOOLED

Early in the summer of 1930, it was generally quoted that brokers had instructed their employees to take their vacations early, because a brisk market was expected in August. The public naturally looked for a young bull market. Instead, during the greater part of the summer we witnessed declining prices. I did not hear of any broker who was not able to keep up with business, and I doubt if many were forced to work their staff's overtime.

It is rather discouraging to some of us to read so many announcements apparently released to fool the public. However, I rather suspect that some of the "big boys" themselves were fooled that summer, as I am certain many of them were quite positive that the inactive weeks in the latter part of May were periods of accumulation. Still, although some were fooled, others fooled the public. One thing is almost as sure as taxes, and that is: that trying to outguess "them" in daily fluctuations is financial suicide for the vast majority. Some may be lucky for a few trades, but not for many more than that. Remember this: the big operators and pool-managers, when successful, outwit or outwait the public. The thing for you and me to do is to try to time our commitments so that we tag along with "them" for the trend (of maybe 1 week, maybe 16 weeks) and precede the public, both in buying and in selling.

And this means not allowing ourselves to be "kidded" into some move, or pushed into following the crowd.

NEVER ANSWER A MARGIN CALL

The Market Philosopher's advice to his class is: *never answer a margin-call.* Tell your broker to sell enough of the shares he is holding for you to meet his requirements. The margin clerk is your best friend: he can be depended upon to tell you when to sell; and if you do not follow his tip, he will sell anyway.

In order to check up on this theory of it's being best never to answer a margin call, I once interviewed a number of brokers. They all, without exception, told me that traders would fare much more profitably than they usually do, if they never replied with more money to protect their margin accounts.

And why should they not?

Your judgment is bound to be biased when your stocks are going against you. It is impossible for you to consider all factors calmly. When you purchased your stocks you expected them to advance. If the opposite movement occurs, your judgment was wrong. Then why, in Heaven's name, throw good money after bad? What is the difference, after all, between a paper loss and an actual loss? Your equity is exactly the same on the broker's books (minus the selling commissions). You are no better off, holding on, than you are if you sell out—in fact, you are not as well situated, because more of your capital is tied up: thus you weaken your position, possibly to the point where you cannot take advantage of whatever bargain prices there may turn up later.

The Danger of Too Much Nerve

I know that there are many who are opposed to the thought I shall expand upon here—that it is dangerous to call upon your nerve to help you stay with a commitment.

Fear is probably the outstanding emotion in the market. (In making these remarks, I have marginal operations in mind.) Although a certain small amount of fear is a wonderful safety-valve, I believe you will agree that any more than that much paralyzes sound reasoning, and that without sound reasoning we have no business speculating.

Let us look at it from another angle: suppose you and I have purchased a certain stock after due deliberation. From our study of the transaction it is our belief that the stock should advance, and, although *minor* reactions (of two or three points, let us say) are to be expected we nevertheless think the *trend* is up. If, instead of advancing, the stock *immediately* reacts (contrary to our previous opinion that reactions were expected *during*, but not *prior* to, the advance), we know that our calculations of the technical position were not accurate. This beclouds the outlook; our original conclusion was erroneously arrived at. If we are confused, or *afraid* of the result, what is the sensible thing to do? Sell; get out and make a new analysis.

Why sell? Why not grit our teeth and say: "By George, I am in this thing and I'll stick it out as long as my money lasts. I've got enough margin to carry it down fifteen more points; I'll show this stock it can't bluff me."

Figure it out for yourself. Perhaps my thinking is askew, but until someone proves to me that it is sounder to use nerve and stick to a commitment which I know, *if I were out of it*—if I were sitting on the sidelines—*I should not buy into*, I am going to continue to be afraid, and can do nothing better than get out. This is a profitable method of reasoning, is it not—to get out of a stock which you would not buy?

I have heard so many traders say, again and again: "I wish I were not long of that stock; if I weren't, believe me, I'd never buy *that* dog." When I ask them why they do not sell, I am informed: "Oh, I can't lose my nerve and sell now; I have a loss in it."

Well, all that I can say is that this shows you one of the many, many reasons why pool operators and professionals make money by trading with the public.

You may reply that, if you sell when in doubt, you may lose a good position. As you know by now, there is, to me, no such thing as "position" in trading. You certainly cannot lose a good position if the position you are in shows you a loss. Likewise, remember, the stock market is not going to close down soon. It will still be there next year, making money for the few who are smart and losing money for the many who are foolish.

Remember: it is not the price you pay for a stock, but the time at which you buy it, which counts in trading.

AVERAGING TO SATISFY PRIDE OF OPINION

Once, in the fall of 1930, when I was on my way to Vermont for a weekend, I ran into an acquaintance in the parlor car. It was not long before our talk swung to the stock market.

He pulled out of his pocket a list of stocks which he had purchased at 1929 near-highs. I listened while he told me of his plans. He said: "I am going to buy more of each of these stocks pretty soon, when I think the bottom has been reached."

I asked him if I might look at his list. I noticed some stocks whose companies were unlikely to prosper to any great extent during the coming year or two. I was naturally interested to learn what prompted his decision to buy more shares of *each* present holding.

"Well, you see, I hate to look at the prices at which I bought these stocks; and if I buy more at these low levels I can average my prices, and I shan't mind so much then. For example, I paid $75 a share for my United Corporation, and if I buy some more at around $20, my average price will only be $47.50, which doesn't look so high."

"Are you going to buy more of every stock regardless of the outlook for the companies? I have no quarrel with your decision on United Corporation, but cannot quite see why you buy more of two or three of your other holdings."

"Oh, yes, i'll buy them all; they're all good stocks."

To my mind, averaging is, in itself, wrong reasoning; but to average simply to satisfy your pride of opinion is financial suicide. In averaging, you are buying *more* of something which is worth *less* than you previously thought it should be worth. When, on the other hand, you buy more of a stock which has advanced *above* what you paid for it, your judgment has been confirmed and your profits are helping you. In averaging down you never know for certain that you are buying at the bottom: a friend of mine averaged Chrysler four times in 1929 and 1930, and the fourth time it was in the eighties!

The fellow who averages at the exact bottom, will immediately rise from his seat and tell me that this theory is all wrong. Perhaps even then it is not wrong, because until the stock has showed him a profit he is not positive that he has not purchased a "sleeper," one which will *stay down*.

CHAPTER 19

ARE CHARTS OF ANY VALUE IN FORECASTING THE MOVEMENTS OF STOCK PRICES?

The interest in stock charts has grown tremendously in the last few years. We find people everywhere keeping them. Upon the slightest excuse they will discuss them, and ask countless questions about them: "What do the charts say today? Does the chart of Steel say to buy it? I see on the chart that Can is a buy; what do you see?"

Obviously, the danger in charts, so often demonstrated by the careless attitude of those who use them, is the temptation to adopt them as a stock market "system" which may be played in just any old lackadaisical fashion, without thought or reason, as one would blindly play a system at Monte Carlo.

Charts do not *say* anything; rather, on them are traced the results of human opinions. Charts do not cause movements in stock prices, but are aids by which trained minds may judge what will be the effect of previous moves.

A. W. Wetsel has done a great deal of important research work in chart theories. I am indebted to him for the little I have learned about charts. He has demonstrated conclusively to me that charts are utterly valueless when employed mechanically—that is, when we go to a chart expecting to find therein an open sesame to market profits.

We all know that stock prices ebb and flow in accordance with the opinions of buyers and sellers. We have learned that stock prices are human conclusions as to values. There are trends of thought in the stock market, exactly as there are in art, literature, and science. These trends of opinion concerning stock values become, in turn, the trends of stock prices. We have the long-term, bull market trend; the intermediate trends, reflecting month-to-month opinions of values and business conditions; and the minor movements resulting from highly speculative opinions of technical market conditions and from the manipulative forces within the market.

When we refer to charts we see pictured the previous trends of traders' and investors' opinions. From these, the analyst, from years of experience in judging the "market mind," is often able to determine whether the balance of opinion is on the buying side or the selling. In other words, he is able to gauge more intelligently the condition of supply and demand. At times we can find recorded upon our charts certain dependable formations which indicate accumulation or distribution of stocks. Trend less markets, which we have when the opinions of buyers and sellers temporarily balance, also may be detected. From chart formations the analyst is able to determine the technical structure—broadly, whether weakness or strength prevails.

In the last analysis, it may be stated that charts are aids, to be used by the intelligent trader or investor, along with many other important means, as guides to market sentiment.

On the other hand, charts are full of dynamite and can cause crushing losses, if blindly followed by the inexperienced who do not realize that, inasmuch as human nature is not constant, there can be no system which is infallible.

Mechanical forecasting will never take the place of intelligent judgment.

CHAPTER 20

FROM MY NOTEBOOK

*   *   *

Pride (of opinion) goeth before a fall (in stock prices).

*   *   *

Do not let the old I-Tell-You-So's fool you with their talk that we are not in a new era, market-wise. Use your own mental equipment and think back only ten years. Do you not think that markets in which millions of the public are interested, may act differently from those in which only two or three hundred thousand professionals operate?

In one, trained individuals keep their fingers on the pulse of affairs; in the other—the present market—the majority of power is in the hands of those with only a sideline interest in the market.

If you do not believe this, think for a moment of the tremendous declines in stock prices during the summer of 1930, when a cataract of liquidation literally poured stocks into the New York stock market to be sold at whatever prices they would bring. Certainly the fact that during the past eight or ten years millions of people have bought stocks for the first time, must be considered when we are trying to estimate the ebb and flow of stock prices.

*   *   *

Never mind telling me *what* stocks to buy;
tell me *when* to buy them.

*   *   *

I shall hazard a forecast: more attention will be paid in the future to an interpretation of human nature as it is affected by economic factors than to the economic factors themselves.

*   *   *

A sale printed on the tape is a meeting of two minds; public sentiment passes in review on the tape for him to read who is schooled in the interpretation of human nature as it is reflected in the stock market.

I often wonder why it is that financial writers try so hard to determine the exact causes behind the action of a certain stock on a given day. Doubtless it is because their readers demand it.

The variety of their interpretations is amazing. It only shows the futility of attempting ever to gauge market movements by published news. Markets pay trifling attention to news after it is out.

*   *   *

Many were called (for margins) but it profited
few to answer.

*   *   *

Within the short space of 15 years the number of investors in common stocks has multiplied 20, perhaps 40, times.

The public is rapidly becoming the owner of industry. Gigantic mergers and holding companies are welding smaller enterprises into huge, centrally managed units, the stocks of which are held by thousands of individuals in every walk of life from that of laborer to that of bank-president.

What will be the result? A safety valve against destructive socialism and communism? Will Labor control Capital through stock ownership of America's leading corporations? Or will Labor become more dissatisfied and demand a larger share of the profits?

Will not the management have to produce results or lose its job, with the consequence that these corporate giants will be all the more efficiently managed—more fairly managed for both stockholders and employees?

It is my thought that the recent "proxy fights" are a mere straw in the wind, that stockholders are paying far more attention to the details of corporate management than some think. I believe that the time is fast passing when the heads of corporations may run affairs to suit their selfish interests. All of which points to pleasanter and more profitable relationships between Capital and Labor.

*   *   *

It is often a long road to the quick turn.

*   *   *

If you would perceive the futility of gauging the trend of stock prices on *judged* valuations, try this:

Ask 10 of your best-posted acquaintances for their opinion of the *value* of the common stock of the General Electric Company. You will, in all probability, receive ten different opinions.

Now let us suppose that you want to sell your stock. What can you get for it? The market price on that day, of course. Does the market price agree with the opinions you received? Again probably not.

Therefore, is not the value of any stock the price at which it may readily be sold? Going one step farther, we come back again to the thought expressed so often in these pages, that to determine the trend of stock prices we must interpret the market's opinion of values, not the judgment of any one group of experts.

*   *   *

Aimless switching gathers no profits.

*   *   *

I am frequently asked to formulate a market plan or program. It is a very difficult thing to do, because everyone is constituted differently, and a program, to be successful, must be in tune with one's temperament. There are many people who should never buy and sell stocks on margin; there are others whose judgment is not affected by marginal trading. Some investors never wish to sell a stock; their purchases, naturally, must differ from those of the individual who has no objection to selling out everything

130

when declining prices are indicated. Common stocks vary widely in their characteristics, and should be fitted to portfolios after a careful analysis of the individual's requirements. The investor or trader, therefore, must plan his program in accordance with his personal prejudices, emotions, desires, temperament, habits, and goal. Both investing and trading are highly specialized, wherein the personal element is perhaps of greater importance than any other factor.

* * *

One profit in cash is worth two on paper.

* * *

The last stages of a rally are at once the most profitable and the most dangerous of all the stages. Rapidly advancing prices, together with increasing volume, are indicative of the end of that movement, or swing. While these price advances are profitable, *if the top is detected in time to sell*, it is undoubtedly more profitable generally to let the other fellow try for the last two or three points. It is a common trait of the amateur speculator that he rushes in with purchase orders when he sees fast action. Too often, however, the market turns over and he is faced with losses.

As one man has said to me: "Do everything in the market opposite to your snap conclusions and contrary to what *appears* logical, and you will probably make money consistently."

* * *

A trendless market is friendless to traders.

* * *

Take it from the Market Philosopher: human nature in the stock market is going to be the most profitable study in the next bull market. The greater the number of traders, the more necessary will it be to study and to know market psychology and have a market philosophy.

Other Investing Classics available at Traders' Library...

The ABC of Stock Speculation
by S.A. Nelson

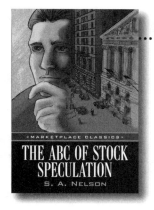

Originally a primer for traders in the early 1900s, this book outlines the history of trading and provides the essentials that still stand true today. Great insight into Dow Theory, market swings, stop orders, from a close friend of Charles Dow. This classic includes original editorials written by Dow himself. A must-have for any investor or trader.

ISBN: 978-1-59280-263-0

$13.50

The Art of Speculation by Philip L. Carret

First published in 1930, this legendary perspective shows what affect speculation, or trading as it is commonly referred to today, has on the markets, business, and the economy this classic has been a mandatory text for any one looking to take money from the markets. Put Carret's insights into value investing, market forecasting, and volatility to work in your trading today and leverage tactics that have stood the test of time.

ISBN: 978-1-59280-261-6

$13.50

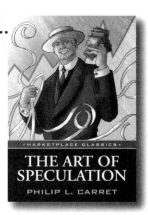

Think and Grow Rich by Napoleon Hill

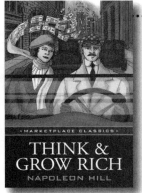

Since its release in 1937, this book has been an influence on more successful people than almost any other title. Written from research in interviews with the industry giants like Thomas Edison, John D. Rockefeller, Alexander Graham Bell, and many others, this guide breaks the path to success into 13 steps. Find out what these steps are and how they can transform you life.

ISBN: 978-1-59280-260-9

$13.50